mockbee

Samuel Mockbee and the Rural Studio:
Community Architecture

Edited by David Moos and Gail Trechsel

This catalogue is published on the occasion of the exhibition
Samuel Mockbee and the Rural Studio: Community Architecture
organized by David Moos at the Birmingham Museum of Art

This exhibition is sponsored by Altria Group, Inc.

Additional support has been provided by:
The Comer Foundation, Interface, Inc., the Rich's Fund of the
Federated Department Stores Foundation and the Graham Foundation

Exhibition schedule:
Birmingham Museum of Art
Birmingham, AL
5 October 2003 to 4 January, 2004

National Building Museum
Washington, DC
22 May to 6 September, 2004

Scottsdale Museum of Contemporary Art
Scottsdale, AZ
25 September, 2004 to 2 January 2, 2005

Published by:
Birmingham Museum of Art
2000 Eighth Avenue North
Birmingham, Alabama 35203
www.artsBMA.org

ISBN 0-931394-52-X

Available through D.A.P./Distributed Art Publishers
155 Sixth Avenue, 2nd Floor, New York, NY 10013
Tel: (212) 627-1999 Fax: (212) 627-9484

Printed and bound in the UK by Butler & Tanner
*(This book has been printed on paper which is 75% recycled from de-inked
post consumer waste using inks which are vegetable based.)*

Art Direction and Design by:
Tom Bejgrowicz/VRA, Birmingham, AL

All Rural Studio photography, unless otherwise indicated,
© Timothy Hursley, all rights reserved.

Additional photography by:
Robert Linthout, M. Sean Pathasema and Cynthia Connolly

Front cover:
(top)
Detail of Samuel Mockbee, *The Black Warrior*, 1996, Oil on canvas
mounted on plywood with wood, found wood, metal and corrugated
metal, beaver sticks, bottles, gourds, garden clipper, string and
tape, 174 x 96 inches. Courtesy Jackie Mockbee and Family.

(bottom)
Rural Studio, *The Lucy House*, Mason's Bend, Hale County, AL,
2001-2002, Outreach Studio Project. Photograph by Timothy
Hursley.

Back cover:
Samuel Mockbee, *Preliminary Sketch: Fabrications, Full Scale
(Elevation with photos)*, 1997, Pen, ink and colored pencil on paper
with photo collage and Duct tape, 14 x 17 inches. Courtesy of Max
Protetch Gallery, New York.

Frontispiece:
(top)
Detail of Samuel Mockbee, *Lizquina: Mother Goddess* also
called *Lucy's Paramour*, 1993–1995, Oil on wood with rubber
tires, tree bark, found wood, metal, lawn mower chain, rope,
beaver sticks and gourd, 114 x 104 inches. Courtesy Jackie
Mockbee and Family.

(bottom)
Rural Studio, *The Yancey Chapel*, Sawyerville, Hale County, AL,
1995, Thesis Project. Photograph by Timothy Hursley.

CONTENTS

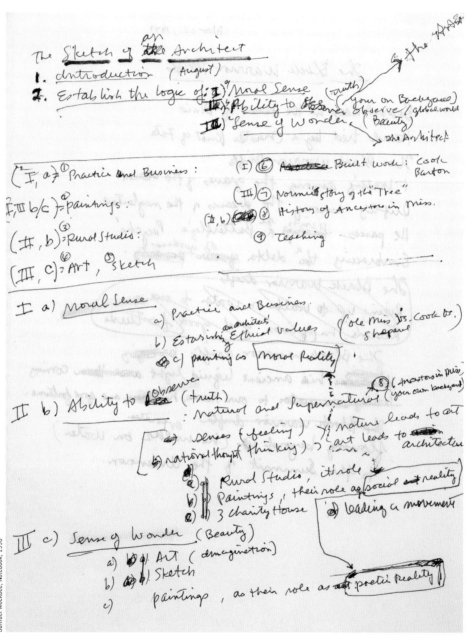

The Sketch of an ~~the~~ Architect ⟶ the ~~Artist~~

1. Introduction (August)
2. Establish the logic of: I) Moral Sense (truth)
   II) Ability to ~~observe~~ Observe / global world (Your on Background)
   III) Sense of Wonder (Beauty)
   ⟶ the Architect

(I, a) ① Practice and Business :   (I) ⑥ ~~Architect~~ Built work : Cook Barton
(I,III b/c) ② Paintings :   (III) ⑦ Normie story of the "Tree"
(II, b) ③ Rural Studio :   (II, b) ⑧ History of Ancestors in Miss.
(III, C) ④ Art, ⑤ Sketch   ⑨ Teaching

I a) Moral Sense
   a) Practice and Business
   b) Establishing an architects' Ethical values   (Ole Miss Is. Shepard (Cook Dr.)
   ⊙ c) painting as [Moral Reality]

II b) Ability to ~~Observe~~ Observe (truth)   ⑧ (Ancestors in Miss, your own backyard)
   : Natural and Supernatural (your own backyard)
      a) senses (feeling)   x) nature leads to art
      b) rational thought (thinking)   art leads to ~~art~~ architecture
         a) a) Rural Studio, it's role
         b) b) Paintings , their role as [social art reality]
         c) c) 3 charity House   d) leading a movement

III c) Sense of Wonder (Beauty)
   a) a) Art (imagination)
   b) b) Sketch   [poetic Reality]
   c)   paintings , as their role as ~~art~~ poetic Reality

INTRODUCTION: A SENSE OF WONDER

Gail Trechsel and David Moos

On one of his notebook pages that bears the heading, "The Sketch of an Architect," Samuel Mockbee set out the parameters through which he defined his creative enterprise:

I   Moral Sense
II   Ability to Observe (truth)
III Sense of Wonder (beauty)[1]

Linking ethical, social, and poetic realities would be Mockbee's fate. At the core of his being, and at the center of his thinking as an architect, was the drive for justice and a mutual respect for all human beings. Mockbee possessed the genial ability to express his moral principles and his ideals of fairness through the creation of buildings of profound beauty. The houses, community centers, churches, meeting pavilions, playgrounds, and other essential structures that he presided over at the Rural Studio both reflect and transcend their cultural context. Inflected by southern vernacular form, Mockbee's inventive design was infused with resourceful construction solutions and unique applications of salvaged, recycled, or reapplied materials. For Hale County, Alabama—a place synonymous with chronic definitions of poverty—Mockbee conceived of architecture as not merely entailing great design, but also encompassing an agenda of social transformation, an organic process of helping people by coming to know them. "What is required," Mockbee asserted, "is the replacement of abstract opinions with knowledge based on real human contact and personal realization applied to the work."[2]

Mockbee's notebooks also diagram his methodology for the Rural Studio, elucidating his belief that each component of the building process is intimately connected with every other. The new strategy that he and D. K. Ruth, chair of the department of architecture at Auburn University, devised for the teaching of architecture stemmed from a desire to make things better—within the discipline of architecture and beyond. They sought to develop a system of instruction that took the students out of the classroom of the university and thrust them into the classroom of the world. Second-year architecture students can elect to spend one quarter at the Rural Studio, working in a group of about fifteen, solving each aspect of what architecture is: from initially meeting with the client in order to determine needs and desires, to the preliminary creative and design phase, to the structural and engineering stage, and finally undertaking actual construction. Fifth-year, or thesis students, spend an entire year working in teams of three or four undertaking projects from inception to completion. In this manner students develop deep working relationships (among themselves and with clients), acquire a better understanding of teamwork and compromise, while learning that design and construction are a continuum. If the Rural Studio was initially concerned with providing houses for disadvantaged Hale County residents, it rapidly increased its scope to provide structures that have reinvigorated, indeed reimagined, the larger social environment.

Mockbee's holistic vision of architecture as pedagogy and social activism developed incrementally. In the late-1970s, after he himself had graduated from Auburn University with a degree in architecture and was practicing in Canton, Mississippi, he began to be troubled by the inequities that still pervaded the South following the Civil Rights movement. The lingering awareness that his own life of opportunity was enabled at the expense of African-Americans in his community began to weigh on his conscience. An occasion to address this concern presented itself in the early 1980s through a Canton housing initiative that sought to renovate existing houses and provide new ones for needy families.

---

[1] Samuel Mockbee, Notebook, 1996. The title page inscription gives the date of each notebook. In many cases Mockbee often later revised or added pages of writing and sketches. All Notebooks are courtesy of Jackie Mockbee and Family.

[2] Randolph Bates, "Interview with Samuel Mockbee," in *Mockbee Coker: Thought and Process*, Lori Ryker, ed. (New York: Princeton Architectural Press, 1995), 99.

Rural Studio, Harris (Butterfly) House, Mason's Bend, Hale County, AL, 1997

As he participated in this enterprise, which provided his first meaningful encounter with poor African-Americans, Mockbee gained essential insight into issues of community, class, and race. He understood that ignorance of "the other" and economic disparity, rather than merely race, were the key characteristics that defined difference. Once Mockbee and those working closely with him crossed into the other world—or to use the phrase that came to symbolize the entry of Auburn students into the lives of Hale County residents, once they "stepped over the threshold"—mutual respect grew and preconceptions abated.

Mockbee would sometimes illustrate lectures about the Rural Studio by showing a slide of a view of Greensboro, Alabama, taken in 1936 by Walker Evans. He would point out that, with the exception of one building that had burned down, the town looked just the same. He would then flash an image of the town taken in the 1990s. "What is sad about the two photographs," Mockbee would say, "is that in those sixty years not a damn thing has changed for some of our citizens and yet we still continue to believe things are getting better, but they are not...."[3] The Rural Studio endeavored to change this picture. Ruth and Mockbee selected Hale County, in the heart of Alabama's Black Belt,[4] located over 100 miles from Auburn's campus, because the majority of residents are mired in a cycle of poverty that dates back to Reconstruction.[5] Here Mockbee could implement the essence of his own epiphany and confer the sense of wonder that architecture-in-action is capable of delivering. As Mockbee led his students on the path to becoming "citizen architects," he defined through his own humanistic and profoundly idealistic vision of responsibility the intersection of architecture with community.

Mockbee's work at the Rural Studio is now internationally known. Following exhibitions at the Max Protetch Gallery, New York; the Contemporary Arts Center, Cincinnati; his posthumous inclusion in the 2002 Whitney Biennial, New York; and the publication of Andrea Oppenheimer Dean's comprehensive, *Rural Studio: Samuel Mockbee and an Architecture of Decency* (2002), Mockbee's undertaking has entered mainstream consciousness. What is often missing from the story of "The Hero of Hale County" (as a feature in *Architectural Record* dubbed Mockbee in its title), however, is the fact that Mockbee was a successful architect who, throughout most of the 1990s, continued to maintain his partnership and professional practice with Coleman Coker in Memphis. In 1995, as the Rural Studio was gaining early maturity, a monograph, *Mockbee Coker: Thought and Process*, published by Princeton Architecture Press, documented the sleek and ambitious private houses that the firm specialized in. Indeed, the so-called Pickwick House, located in Shiloh Falls, Tennessee, was not only featured on the cover of *Architectural Record* but also appeared in several coffee-table volumes such as *The New American House 2: Innovation in Residential Design and Construction* (1997) and *Modern House 2* (2000).

The strength of Mockbee's professional abilities makes his commitment to the Rural Studio all the more poignant. Mockbee was an architect who could easily have continued on a career path catering to wealthy clients. Instead, he chose, with Emersonian idealism, to embark on an untested project, to make pedagogy the conceptual center of his practice. The kind of knowledge that Mockbee discovered with his students in Hale County can only be lived. Bold is the idea of providing homes for the disenfranchised residents of Hale County; more radical, however, is the commitment to having undergraduate students assume responsibility for the entire architectural process. Both these moves define the essence of empowerment, and it took great courage for Mockbee to pursue his convictions. Early on, he knew what was at stake. In a 1994 notebook, the frontispiece, which Mockbee inscribed using a quill pen and his finest grandiose script, he inscribed the following: "Rural Studio / Greensboro, Alabama / January 1994 / 'I will fight until I die against the cruelty of small ambition.' Anon. – (a friend of W. B. Yeats from his boyhood)."[6] Such words,

---

[3] Quoted from Mockbee's lecture, Rotary Club of Birmingham, January 31, 2001.

[4] "The Black Belt, [is] a multicounty crescent of geography named in the early nineteenth century for its soil but soon, and as frequently, identified with its large African American population....In the 1850s the Black Belt of Alabama was one of the richest regions of plantation slavery in America. During the twentieth century, the effects of generations of soil erosion combined with the invasion of the boll weevil and the collapse of the cotton market all but destroyed the region's row crop farming." See Allen Tullis, "Alabama Bound, Unbound," in Trudy Wilner Stack, *Christenberry Reconstruction: The Art of William Christenberry* (Jackson: University Press of Mississippi, 1996), 14.

[5] The twelve-county Black Belt of Alabama ranks near the bottom of the nation in most major statistical categories such as Poverty, Infant Deaths, Quality of Education and Healthcare, Births to Single Mothers, Unemployment, and Life Expectancy. For a comprehensive analysis, see the special series of reports "The Black Belt: Alabama's Third World," *The Birmingham News*, May 12, 2002, 1A, 11A-14A.

[6] Samuel Mockbee, Notebook, 1994.

Rural Studio, Mason's Bend Community Center, Mason's Bend, Hale County, AL, 2000

hinting at battles to be fought, tell of the stamina required to launch, nurture, and maintain the Rural Studio—perhaps the most audacious, innovative, and effective architecture program in the United States.

This exhibition at the Birmingham Museum of Art began when Samuel Mockbee was initially engaged to mount what would become the major exhibition of his work with the Rural Studio. As dates were discussed and preliminary decisions made, the project acquired additional focus. Mockbee and the Rural Studio would make a proposal to improve the museum's outdoor sculpture garden by building a structure that would rebuff incessant noise from nearby Interstate 20. A rough model was built and preparatory thinking commenced. The sculpture garden project was to be the monumental built component of the exhibition. An exhibition tour would be organized, a catalog produced, and a great opening party would be given at the museum.

Two projects preoccupied Mockbee as he lay dying in a hospital room in Jackson, Mississippi, late-December 2001. One was his submission to an exhibition of architects' responses to the World Trade Center attacks of September 11, 2001; the other was a major building expansion of the Birmingham Museum of Art. Mockbee had recently agreed to take on this project and to make a proposal for what would have become his largest undertaking. The project—of expanding Alabama's premier art museum for the twenty-first century—appealed to him because it could exemplify the diverse motives of his imagination and intellect. In the final conversation, Mockbee said that he would make an ambitious, challenging design proposal. "If you don't like it," he said, preempting concessions, "we won't dance, no hard feelings." There are few words with which to capture the fact that Mockbee died at the true height of his creative powers, poised at the threshold of doing truly great deeds that could affect the course of a city, reshape an entire rural environment.

This exhibition embodies our gratitude to Samuel Mockbee for the work that he did accomplish and the ingenious solutions he set in motion. His vision was durable as is amply evidenced by the projects featured in the Appendix of Rural Studio Projects 2001-2003 included in this publication and spanning the time since his death. Some of these most recent projects represent a new level of ambition and emphasis upon craftsmanship, attesting to the Rural Studio's ability to have built upon the strong foundation of Mockbee's germinal vision. Mockbee's creative breadth was protean: he circumscribed the scope of the Rural Studio's enterprise through painting, drawing, and poetry. These other media are abundantly represented in this exhibition and vividly portray the unique scope of his inspiration. His paintings are especially powerful renditions of the relationships that he shared with clients of the Rural Studio and of the attachment that he felt for Hale County—the verdant, at times mesmerizing landscape, almost overdetermined by its history.

This exhibition would not have been possible without the substantial support of Altria Group, Inc. Additional support has been provided from the Comer Foundation, the Rich's Fund of the Federated Department Stores Foundation, and the Graham Foundation. Special thanks are due Max Protetch and Josie Browne of the Max Protetch Gallery, New York. Jackie Mockbee and her family have loaned numerous paintings and the notebooks of Samuel Mockbee to this exhibition and for their willingness to do so we are grateful. Many of these works have never before been on view. Without the definitive photographs of Timothy Hursley and his willingness to accommodate our many requests, this publication would not have been possible.

We are grateful to all contributors—fellow architects, students, artists, critics, friends of Sambo's (as he was known to those closest to him)—who answered our call for submissions. The varied appraisals and homages form a vivid tribute to an irreplaceable man. Each individual contribution elaborates upon an aspect of Mockbee, from his larger-than-life personality to the inclusive idealism that he implemented at the Rural Studio. Only such a multiplicity of perspectives can begin to adequately circumscribe the nuances of Mockbee's complex contribution to architecture. VRA has expertly fit the many pieces of this puzzle together and produced an excellent catalog. Finally, our thanks are due to Andrew Freear, the key collaborator who has made realization of this exhibition possible. Like the students who helped Andrew prepare for this exhibition and install it in our galleries, he incarnates the best of Mockbee—enthusiasm, innovation, and a true sense of wonder. ■

Samuel Mockbee's painting studio, Canton, MS. Photographed 2003

Samuel Mockbee: The Architect as Painter

David Moos

"For me, drawing and painting are the initial influences for the making of architecture." —*Samuel Mockbee*

Samuel Mockbee's painting studio was unique. On the lawn in front of the angular corrugated metal-clad house that he designed and built for himself and his family in Canton, Mississippi, he erected an open-air studio. With its metal roof held aloft by tall pillars and its bare earthen floor, this space was simple. Exposed to the elements on all sides and surrounded by the flat greenness of the lawn, the structure was sheltered only by the large oak tree beneath which it is situated. While he painted, Mockbee could watch his children roam the lawn or play basketball nearby. The studio was an archetypal Mockbee space: a realm in which to focus the imagination; immersed in the landscape to convene with nature; an accessible and open place where friends could pull up a chair and visit—a space for interaction.

This studio, which is perhaps the architect's most rudimentary and personal structure, informs how one might approach Mockbee's work—his defining contributions to the fields of architecture, pedagogy, social activism, and painting. It is, in fact, through painting that Mockbee articulated his aspirations for all of these expressive domains. In the early 1990s, as the Rural Studio was beginning to take form, Mockbee created what he referred to as murals— very large, boldly colored paintings that invited viewers to become participants. Works like *The Children of Eutaw Pose before Their Ancient Cabin* (1992) function as an actual painted environment, offering shelter while simultaneously serving as a mythical threshold. Children could enter the painting's portals and metaphorically reconnect with their atavistic history. The title suggests that the work is only properly functioning when children are present. On a page in one of his notebooks, Mockbee envisions the portals of his mural as existing in an Edenic context, attended to by benign animal creatures and a majestic, magical tree with foliage the color of peacock feathers.

Notebook sketch after *The Children of Eutaw Pose Before their Ancient Cabins*, 1995. Ink, graphite, felt marker, collage and photo-collage on glossy paper, 7 x 9 inches

The Children of Eutaw Pose Before their Ancient Cabins, installed in Eutaw, AL, 1993

Lizquina: Mother Goddess also called *Lucy's Paramour*, 1993–1995
Oil on wood with rubber tires, tree bark, found wood, metal, lawn mower chain, rope, beaver sticks and gourd, 114 x 104 inches

Mockbee's assertion that architecture, if it was to express something profound about place, had to proceed from knowledge of that place commenced with drawing and painting. For him, pictorial reality was the essential foundation to the built world. Painting was a means of familiarization, exploration, and invocation. Indeed, for Mockbee, a fifth-generation Mississippian who grew up in Meridian, was educated at Auburn University in Alabama, and made his home in Canton, Mississippi, painting allowed him to plumb the mythical depths of the Deep South. Painting served as a means through which he could narrativize history, envision an ideal present, and commute between real and imagined versions of the world.

In another mural, *Lizquina: Mother Goddess* (1993-1995),[1] Mockbee presents a fiery female deity ascending skyward, borne aloft on flaming wings. Her red body, which diagonally traverses the composition, is crowned by a head composed from painted tree bark and a shredded tire backed by collaged slats of wood. Beaver sticks (a favorite Mockbee material) attached to the surface become three-dimensional vectors that accentuate the visual movement of this composition. The one horizontally placed stick allows Mockbee to affix other materials such as the tangled rope that surrounds the neck of the figure along the right edge of the painting. A painted gourd and two long black curving lengths of a lawn mower chain are additional real-world elements that Mockbee has incorporated into his visionary painting.

The tension between the realness of objects and their transformation into the realm of painting is made evident when one considers that Mockbee first installed this work in a forest glade. Propped up on wood and cinder-block supports, this mural tested whether painting could survive in the landscape, whether its figures and narratives could cross from the domain of pictorial representation and exist in the physical world. This play between fantasy and reality addresses a central trope in Southern consciousness: the uneven boundary between truth and fiction.[2] It is, presumably, for this reason that Mockbee relies upon collage and assemblage. By incorporating objects that are preinscribed with significance (beaver sticks, tires, chains, rope, etc.) into the painting, Mockbee seeks to bring the world of familiar experience—which has often been defined through hardship and inequity—into contact with an inspirational mythical world.

In a notebook entry Mockbee reveals his aspiration. To him the role of painting was to express "truth, beauty, and a moral sense, place," and to establish an artistic character rooted in the vernacular and the universal. His eloquence about painting is profound, telegraphed in terse penned thoughts:

Style: composition of the painting a) silhouette b) form c) detail d) color
Memory: to evoke the viewer's ability to remember or relate to the subject matter; i.e. universal memory and local memory
Delivery: establish a common ground between religion and philosophy and between nature and human nature and greatness and goodness[3]

Now when one considers the murals installed in the landscape, functioning outdoors and enduring, as Mockbee noted, "all sorts of bad weather,"[4] the gesture acquires poignancy: they are envoys that seek to connect the landscape with

---

[1] Mockbee later changed the title of this painting to *Lucy's Paramour*, which is indicative of how he used his paintings to elaborate relationships that he shared with his architectural clients.

[2] "Sadly, for the most part, the South's past has more affection for fiction and false values than it does for facing the truth. Fortunately, in my lifetime, the suffering and brutality attached to those false values have been challenged by people with the courage to accept responsibility." Randolph Bates, "Interview with Samuel Mockbee," in *Mockbee Coker: Thought and Process*, Lori Ryker, ed. (New York: Princeton Architectural Press, 1995), 93.

[3] Samuel Mockbee, Notebook, 1995.

[4] Bates, "Interview with Samuel Mockbee," op. cit., 101.

Worms for Sale, 1999. Oil, dirt, cardboard, paper, rubber tires, glove, wood, wire, twigs, ceramic fragments and dental mould on Masonite with painted wood stretcher, 61 x 39 inches

human decency; offerings intended to elicit the good in citizens of the Deep South and, perhaps, inspire greatness.

These are lofty, grandiloquent terms for painting. Were Mockbee not able to implement his agenda of social activism through architecture and pedagogy, the ambitions he set for his painting might seem outsized. Taken in the context of his oeuvre, however, painting does indeed hold out the potential to proffer a transformative experience. In this regard Mockbee's painting relates to that of Robert Rauschenberg, the artist with whom he maintains an essential conversation. When one sees the black tire in Lizquina or a similarly shredded tire collaged atop another Mockbee painting titled *Worms for Sale* (1999), the image of Rauschenberg's *Monogram* (1955-59) is summoned. In that work, one of Rauschenberg's well-known Combines, he redefined painting as assemblage, placing a rubber tire around the midsection of a stuffed Angora goat that stood in the center of his horizontally oriented painted and collaged canvas. In another Combine painting, *Canyon* (1959), a bald eagle occupies the lower register of the composition, its spread wing feathers frozen in an almost painterly gesture. And *Odalisk* (1955/1958), a freestanding Combine, is crowned by a striding Plymouth Rock rooster. These Rauschenberg works that prominently incorporate three-dimensional stuffed animals changed the parameters of American painting both formally and conceptually.

Although the conventional understanding of Rauschenberg's audacious work of the 1950s concerns a dethroning of the then-dominant Abstract Expressionist mode of painting, another reading, concerning the presence of animals and the aspiration of art to relate to all beings, might also be put forth. Such a possibility appealed to Mockbee. His work is populated by creatures whose presences vitally inform his painting. The turtle, upon whose shell great human burdens are borne, the cat, and birds are recurrent animals featured in Mockbee's pictorial world. In the notebook drawing incorporating *The Children of Eutaw...*, a kinship with Rauschenberg's work is implied through the bird-like animal that presides over the collaged photographic image of the children alighting in the portals of the painting. This curious winged creature appears to possess the skull of the goat from *Monogram* and the spread wings of the black eagle from *Canyon*. Here, the animal presence assumes the form of an artistic link—embracing the radical Combine aesthetic, while also implicitly acknowledging the unique spirit of Rauschenberg's inclusive, collaborative strategy as artist.[5]

Samuel Mockbee, Horn Island, MS, Fall 2001

Mockbee always understood that his task—redressing the unfairness of the South's history through an architecture program that seeks to transform the social order—would be multifaceted. In an early *Self-Portrait* (1976), Mockbee sees himself as fulfilling more than one role. In this work the viewer must constantly appraise what the differences are between his various versions of self. The two large depictions of his face that dominate the composition suggest that Mockbee, the young architect, and Mockbee, the painter, are extremely close. By rendering both likenesses through photography and pencil, and interposing the two media, Mockbee collapses difference while recognizing the two distinct impulses within his being. Along the bottom edge of the paper he has collaged two sets of four small photo-booth portraits. In casual clothes and wearing a necktie, Mockbee proposes some diffident inclinations: quizzical, grave, concerned, daunted (in one frame his back is turned to the camera and in another he cut himself out of the photo).

[5] In the postwar era Rauschenberg is one of the most important artist-activists. His famous undertaking, Rauschenberg Overseas Culture Interchange (ROCI), brought Rauschenberg and his art into dialogue and collaboration with artists and audiences in eleven countries. A more in-depth comparison between Mockbee's work and Rauschenberg's beckons. Links between such works as Mockbee's *Children of Eutaw...* and Rauschenberg's *Minutiae* (1954), created as a stage set for the Merce Cunningham Dance Company, demand to be explored.

Alberta's Ascension, 1999, oil on paper, in salvaged wood frame, 99 x 73 inches

Alberta, 1998. Ink, graphite, crayon, felt marker, metallic ink and watercolor on paper, 14 x 11 inches

These smaller images recall Andy Warhol's four-frame photo-booth strips of film that survey facial expressions, or the documentary use of photography employed by Conceptual artists such as Vito Acconci.

The *Self-Portrait* reveals an introspective Mockbee intuiting his destiny. Mockbee will become an architect who makes unprecedented investments into the relationships that he shares with his clients. Not only will he become intimately familiar with their needs and desires in order to better inform his and his students' building process, but he will also fathom the character of his clients through painting. In works such as *Alberta's Ascension* (1999), Mockbee depicts the wheelchair-bound Alberta Bryant—together with Shepard Bryant, recipient of the Rural Studio's first house—attended to by a benign deity. This chicken-footed, nude, fleshy emissary from the beyond who clasps Alberta's hand in a gesture of solidarity, is another rendition of the deity first portrayed in *Lizquina: Mother Goddess*. Contrary to the fury of that earlier work, *Alberta's Ascension* is pervaded by a sense of calm. Now the blazing wings have been converted into a regal red cape. Birds perch on the deity's shoulder and foliage sprouts from her tree-bark visage. As Albert's wheelchair rides upon the shell of tortoise, this deity mediates between the human and animal realms, joining both in a painterly union.

Defined through its overt embrace of Expressionist color (say, Wassily Kandinsky's green, Franz Marc's blue, Chaim Soutine's red), its recollection of the fragrant, faraway exoticism encountered by Paul Gauguin, and its willingness to engage the mystical yearnings of Frantisek Kupka or Ferdinand Hodler, Mockbee's painted world is one of magical dimensions. Adversity is vanquished, as figures like Alberta Bryant are ennobled through the presence of art. Indeed, the radicality of Mockbee's murals, installed in the actual landscape to elicit human and animal participation, suggests that painting might function as a stage set for real action. Mockbee seems to have taken the southern folk artist's predilection for transforming found materials and applied it to the social sphere, introducing painting into the lives of the people he cared about deeply. Collage, the formal strategy that he often applied, becomes the metaphor for how painting was inserted into the creative process of architecture. The layers of Mockbee's imagination are distinct but inseparable. "I'm an architect and I'm also a painter," he stated: "That is my passion—to be responsible to the creative process."[6] Painting was his personal means of expressing the aspirations of the Rural Studio—extending the reach of its potential to encompass an ideal world. ■

NOTE:
Titles: Mockbee rarely inscribed titles on his paintings. Based on his notebooks it is sometimes possible to determine a specific title for a painting. Where a title attribution has been made, the title appears in square brackets.
Sketch: The term sketch is used to designate a page from one of Mockbee's bound notebooks.
Dating: Based on notebook entries it is possible to ascribe accurate dates to many of Mockbee's paintings and drawings that are undated on either recto or verso.
All works are Courtesy Jackie Mockbee and Family

[6] Quote in Andrea Oppenheimer Dean, "The Hero of Hale County: Sam Mockbee," *Architectural Record*, (February 2001), 82.

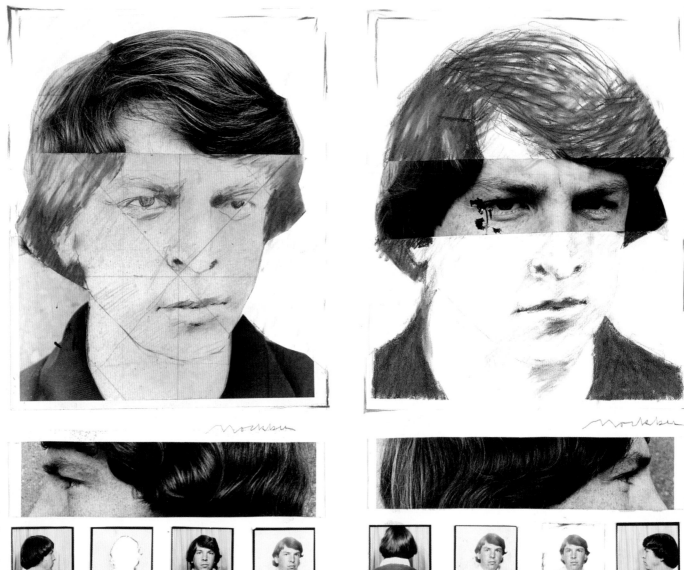

Notebook sketch [*El[quiney or Elschiz – serpent eater*], 1997. Ink, crayon, colored pencil and watercolor on paper, 11 x 14 inches

21

The Black Warrior, 1996, Oil on canvas mounted on plywood with wood, found wood, metal and corrugated metal, beaver sticks, bottles, gourds, garden clipper, string and tape, 174 x 96 inches

2000 Eighth Avenue North
Birmingham, AL 35203-2278
Tel 205.254.2565
Fax 205.254.2714
www.artsBMA.org

MBUSREMUMₒ HₐARMT
MUₒSREMUₒMₒ ₒFₒ ARₜT

15 April 2003

Contributor
Street
City and State

Dear Contributor,

The Birmingham Museum of Art is organizing the exhibition *Samuel Mockbee and the Rural Studio: Everyday Architecture*, the first comprehensive exhibition to survey Mockbee's work with the Rural Studio. This exhibition, which opens in Birmingham on October 3, 2003, and will travel to the National Building Museum, Washington, DC, and the Scottsdale Museum of Contemporary Art, Scottsdale, AZ, will be accompanied by a catalogue that gathers viewpoints and opinions about Mockbee's achievement in architecture, pedagogy and fine art. As editor of this catalogue, which will be distributed by Distributed Art Publishers, I am asking a diverse group of authors from a range of disciplines—spanning architecture, criticism, theory, art, etc.—to contribute short commentaries, appraisals, homages, critiques, and remembrances. I would very much like for you to contribute any thoughts or ideas about Mockbee's work to this publication.

Each writer will be given the same space in the catalogue. Rather than impose a word limit, I am offering you one two-page spread in the catalogue. The individual page size is 10 x 10 inches; thus the actual spread measures 10 x 20 inches. Whatever you choose to submit will be scaled to this spread size and published. Text and images will be printed as specified by authors. The longer the text, the smaller the type-size. Approximately 30 authors have been asked to participate in this publication.

I would greatly appreciate if you could send to me your contribution no later that July 1, 2003, by e-mail or post if required.

This catalogue is intended to compliment Andrea Oppenhimer Dean's monograph, *Samuel Mockbee and an Architecture of Decency* (Princeton Architectural Press, 2002), which is the definitive reference book on Mockbee's work with the Rural Studio. It is also intended to celebrate and appraise the extraordinary contribution of a man who died at the height of his creative abilities.

I thank you in advance for your generous participation in this project. Please be sure to enclose a very brief biographical statement, no longer than 100 words, about yourself.

Sincerely yours,

Dr. David Moos
Curator of Modern and Contemporary Art

dmoos@artsBMA.org

PERSPECTIVES
Thirty points of view on Samuel Mockbee and the Rural Studio

JOE ADAMS
G. WILLIAMSON "B.B." ARCHER
STEVE BADANES
RANDY BATES
JENNIFER BONNER
DAVID BUEGE
WILLIAM CHRISTENBERRY
JOSH C. COOPER
ANDREA OPPENHEIMER DEAN
PAULA DEITZ
BILL DOOLEY
JOHN FORNEY
FRANK GEHRY
ROBERT IVY
BRUCE LANIER
KERRY LARKIN AND LUCY HARRIS
WILLIAM LEVINSON
ATELIER VAN LIESHOUT
BRUCE LINDSEY
LUCY R. LIPPARD
BEATRIZ MILHAZES
RUSHTON AND JAMES PATTERSON
RICHARD I. PIGFORD
CHARLES REEVE
LARRY RINDER
WILLIAM A. RYAN
JAY SANDERS
JEREMY TILL AND SARAH WIGGLESWORTH
RUARD VELTMAN

A Man With
A Boyheart.

My dear friend, Sambo Mockbee, never outgrew his boyheart. Thankfully. It served him well. He was fun-loving, imaginative, curious about all things creative. He was totally unpretentious and down to earth. He liked "authentic" things and tended to categorize everything as either authentic or fake. He was a true "Child of the South" and remained so until his passing.

Sambo had a Southern heart which bound us together from the moment we met. We were instant buddies.

I had contacted him somewhat out of the blue. I had read about him and his architecture long before he founded the Rural Studio. I'm no authority on architecture, but I admire his work. So I wrote to him before a business trip to Jackson. (My secretary said it was the dumbest letter I had ever dictated. I told him I was coming to Mississippi to give a speech, to eat a mess of catfish, and to meet him. I suggested that we could perhaps eat some catfish together and talk. He called right away and we set a date.)

We had a lot in common other than a love for catfish. We both had three daughters; we both had married at an early age while still in college. We both knew Son Thomas, the black folk artist and blues musician. Sambo loved Son's music; I loved his strange gumbo clay heads. We talked about revelations that had changed our lives. We talked about our favorite writers, and they were all Southerners.

Sambo gave me a whirlwind tour of homes he had designed. And, at each place, he was welcomed like the Prodigal Son returning. His clients adored him.

Sambo loved the rural landscape. Tractor sheds, barns, silos --- they gave him inspiration for his designs.

He insisted that he was a Southern architect. I insisted that he was an architect who lived in the South; that great design knows no geography. (I felt I had won this argument a few years later when two of Sambo's homes were selected for inclusion in a book, GLOBAL ARCHITECTURE, when only seven American homes in total were selected.)

Sambo came to believe that I had been "sent to him". He

began calling me St. Joe. It made me laugh. I told him he would have trouble finding anyone else to testify to my sainthood. But he just shrugged and said he didn't need any testifying. He kept calling me St. Joe, and it wasn't a joke to him. One day the thought came to me that saints aren't born; they have to earn their sainthood. So maybe I was a saint in the making. Something I had said or did had changed him. He promised to tell me but never did. I suspect it was because I preached that people needed the courage to follow their hearts no matter what. And I suspect that Sambo knew he should be teaching. It was his calling. He was in love with the art and humanity of architecture, not the business of architecture.

But his vision was not teaching in a regular classroom. When he and D.K. Ruth co-founded the Rural Studio, his vision was to completely immerse students in a life-altering learning experience --- to take them out of the classroom and into one of the poorest counties in Alabama.

I feel blessed to have been invited to the Rural Studio from the very beginning. It was a phenomenal atmosphere --- a dozen or more students living for a semester in an old abandoned mansion in Greensboro. They were there not just to study architecture. They were on a mission to design and build a house for a poor family. They had very limited financial resources. They had to use their imagination; scrounge for building materials. And they had to do the physical work of construction.

Sambo insisted that they treat the poor black families with great respect; treat them as a "client". They had to interview them and learn about what the families needed and desired. He told them a good home had to be "warm, dry and noble. It has to lift the spirits."

It was the first time most of these students had every come face-to-face with real poverty. Unless you have been to the community of Mason's Bend, you might not know what true poverty looks like...and smells like.

Their first client was an old black couple in Mason's Bend. The house they were living in was nothing but a shack. It had dirt floors. The roof leaked and flooded the inside of the house.

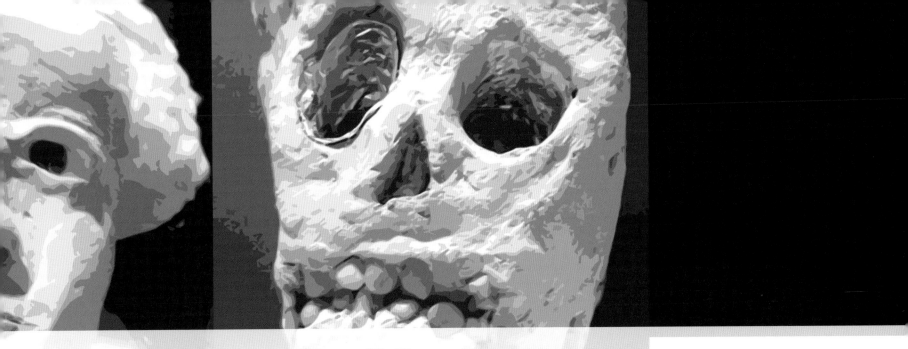

The adjacent pigpen filled the air with a constant, noxious odor (unless you were a pig or a pig farmer). The old man tried to build a new house. He couldn't lift the heavy sheets of wallboard so he had broken the 4x8 sheetrock into small pieces...then he would carry the pieces to the new site and try to piece them back together. The Auburn students arrived just in time!

Before I came on my first visit, Sambo had me re-read Joseph Conrad's HEART OF DARKNESS. Also James Agee and Walker Evans book, LET US NOW PRAISE FAMOUS MEN. They were required reading for the students and very appropriate for being in Hale County where little had changed for the poor blacks since the Depression.

Sambo wasn't just teaching architecture. He was submerging his students in the humanities. They had their meals together around a huge table they constructed. They prayed before meals. They had lively discussions after dinner about what they were reading, what they were studying. Students had to learn classical and historical forms of architecture renderings (creating designs using watercolors that often required exacting overlays of 20 or 25 brushstrokes to achieve a certain color). One other time when I visited, Sambo had brought a truckload of beaver sticks to Greensboro. (Beaver sticks are pieces of limbs that have the bark chewed off by beavers and then is bleached by the sun. Sambo loved beaver sticks. He used them in his art. He used them as ink pens. He would sharpen the points, dip them in an ink bottle and write artful, calligraphy-like letters, albeit short letters. But each letter was a work of art. And his language was elegant and brilliant, reminiscent of another time. In fact, Sambo was convinced that he was a reincarnated general from the Confederacy --- and his writing style made his thought believable.

For the second coming of St. Joe , students had to design and build a chair with beaver sticks. He had warned them that I was a "big saint" and that I was going to sit on each chair. If a chair fell through, the student would get an "F" on their project. When I arrived, fifteen magnificent chairs were sitting on the lawn. Sambo had told the students I was an art dealer so one of the young women had also made an easel to sit by the chair. And none of the chairs fell through.

As part of students' education, Sambo had visitors in at least once a week to have dinner and talk to the students. He had poets, musicians, craftsmen. He greatly admired craftsmanship in all forms. He included beautiful woodworking and custom made furniture into the homes he designed and he wanted the students to know that attention to detail was the essence of a great design.

My role at the Rural Studio was to "preach." Sambo thought it was amusing that I had a Doctorate of Divinity degree which I got through the mail for ten dollars. (As I told Sambo, "you can get some good stuff through the mail.)

He would say, "Tell them what they need to know" as if I had the wisdom of the ages. I would tell them things like: "Never work for bastards. Or be one." "Enthusiam is just as important as talent. If you are enthusiastic you can learn to do anything." "Creativity is a way of living; a way of being."

My sermons were so well received that Sambo took to calling on me to preach with him at meetings of architectural societies. He called these sessions "Sambo Mockbee's Gospel Hour". We had black gospel choruses perform with us. By then, I was wearing a priest's collar and a monsignors hat so I looked authentic to the unsuspecting audience. My wife said we would both get stuck by lightening and go straight to hell. But Sambo told her he thought God had a great sense of humor. I sure hope so. I was basically the warm-up act for Sambo who would then preach about architecture. He got standing ovations wherever he went, including the New York Society of Architects.

Sambo filled his students with a passion that will last them for a lifetime. No one wanted to leave the Rural Studio when the semester ended. Some came back after college to teach with Sambo.

I visited the Rural Studio twice recently. And I am happy to report that Sambo's spirit is alive and well. Throughout his teaching he admonished students: "Proceed,...and be BOLD." It has become the mantra.

– *Joe Adams*

B.B. Archer / Sally Archer   Sambo Mockbee / Jackie Mockbee

SAMBO

"The Big Mock," I have never known anyone like him. Sambo was my best friend. We knew each other for 43 years. Someone once said "to win without risk is to triumph without glory." Sambo stretched his spirit and reached outside the envelope of traditional thought and moved in the only direction available to him. His art, indeed his creative mind, was frustrated by the restrictions of customary practice and artistic convention. His whole being was rooted in the deep South. Its complexities and contradictions fueled his imagination. His vision never found closure, he was curious to his earthly end.

He was a very spiritual man without being religious. He had a sincere belief that one should give of what one has, not material but what lies deep within ones soul. He was more fun and made me laugh more than anyone I ever knew. It makes me glad to see him receive so many accolades. He deserved them all. He stayed the course. I once introduced Sambo to an audience comprised of mostly people he knew from his youth. On that day, I introduced him as follows: "An artistic Bedouin, whose home is the deep South, who knows no prouder title than his name, whose only conceivable honor is his own. His art integral to self, his genius: intuitive truth."

Sambo had a dream for all those many years. He never lost it. Today that dream is a legacy that manifests itself in his Rural Studio, its students, past and present, his wonderful wife and children, his many friends and his best friend. I loved Sambo. I will miss him always. You see "the Big Mock" was a fine man, a mighty fine man. So, Bo, as we often said together: "Here's to us, them's like us, damn few left."

– G. Williamson "B.B." Archer
  Friend and fellow Architect

June 30, 2003

**University of
Washington**

Department of
ARCHITECTURE

College of Architecture & Urban
Planning
208 Gould Hall . Box 355720
Seattle, WA 98195-5720

206.543.4180
FAX: 206.616.4992

<depts.washington.edu/archdept>

Dr. David Moos
Birmingham Museum of Art
200 Eighth Avenue North
Birmingham, AL 35203

Dear Dr. Moos,

It is an honor to be invited to contribute to the catalogue for "Samuel Mockbee and the Rural Studio: Everyday Architecture." I've been thinking about this responsibility for awhile – and the deadline is at hand, so I'll give it a try. When the MacArthur Foundation asked me to write a letter it was really easy – for several reasons:

1. Sambo was still alive
2. He really needed the money!
3. Only a few people would get to read what I wrote!

This assignment seems to embody greater responsibility and the results will hang around a lot longer and have a much larger audience. Some contributors will no doubt recount what Sambo achieved. Others will speculate on what he might have achieved had things worked out differently, and all will attempt to determine his legacy. As a friend and fellow educator, I'd like to focus on what he taught.

There are many architects with exceptional creativity, however most are content to channel that creativity into design – usually in the service of the tiny percentage of the population that can afford it. Sambo taught his students not only to be visionary designers, but to be social, political and environmental visionaries as well.

The Rural Studio's innovative use of common and recycled materials – tires, hay bales, rammed earth, and carpet squares – stands in marked contrast to corporate architecture's materials palette (it's fairly common for instance, to see marble quarried in Vermont – shipped to Italy to be sliced into slabs – then shipped back here and slapped onto a skyscraper in Houston which is air conditioned and lit 24 hours a day and 60% occupied eight hours a day!) We're beginning to realize that "progress" has resulted in construction materials with high embodied energy, high maintenance requirements, short life spans, and which are often toxic and pollute the environment both during their production and during transport to building sites. The Rural Studio has led the way in the use of imaginative "earth-friendly" materials.

As social visionaries, the Rural Studio's commitment to public service, community based projects and to working for those who do not normally have access to architecture is a lesson to us all. Dedication to vernacular traditions, community involvement and sustainable design and technology have left their mark on all the built work of the Studio.

And it's changed the world as well. The world has beaten a path to the tiny town of Newbern, Alabama, and the Rural Studio has had a powerful impact on how architects are educated. By combining hands-on-construction experience with real world needs, the studio has provided a life transforming experience for the students involved and for the families that benefit from their work.

In the early 90's architectural education was becoming more theoretical and abstract and drifting from its roots in construction. With the advent of programs like the Rural Studio, students at other schools are pressing for more hands-on design build and socially and environmentally responsible programs. Hopefully these values will extend into their careers as practitioners as well.

Several years ago, Doctors without Borders received the Nobel Peace Prize. The Rural Studio is one of the few parallels in the field of architecture. A handful of students in a town no one can find on the map have sent a strong message to a profession that has traditionally reserved its accolades for high profile "superstar" architects working with stratospheric budgets for wealthy clientele. Your influence is like your shadow or the ripple of a pebble thrown into the Black Warrier River – it extends out to where you've never been!

Two weeks ago I received word that another friend – also an artist/architect/educator – Doug Michels, co-founder of the Ant Farm collaborative, died in a fall in Australia several weeks before his 60th birthday. The similarities were amazing. Both Sambo, and Doug were heroes and a source of inspiration to all that met them. Both were fabulous storytellers, teachers and lovers of life! They were both off the charts in terms of imagination, intelligence, exuberance, and the ability to make people, particularly students, feel better about themselves. And both were always totally positive and calm in any situation and could make you laugh til you could barely stand. Their energy, attitude, and vision were so necessary in today's world and it's a tragedy for architecture that we lost them so early when many who embody the worst values of the profession practice on into senility (no names provided here)!

Samuel Mockbee was an inspiration as an architect, teacher, and human being. The profession has lost a visionary leader, but his work with the Rural Studio remains as a jumping off point. The program continues and students taught by Sambo will continue to multiply his influence for years - that's the beauty of education!

Thanks for the opportunity to contribute!

XOX

Steve Badanes

Yay, Den 2

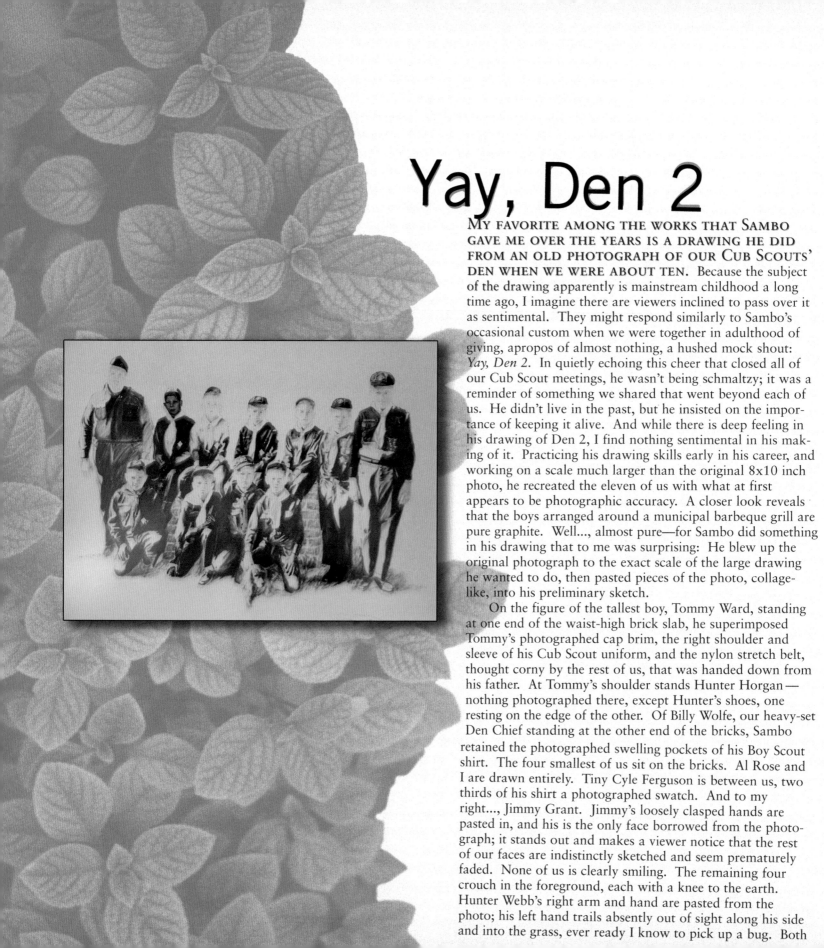

MY FAVORITE AMONG THE WORKS THAT SAMBO GAVE ME OVER THE YEARS IS A DRAWING HE DID FROM AN OLD PHOTOGRAPH OF OUR CUB SCOUTS' DEN WHEN WE WERE ABOUT TEN. Because the subject of the drawing apparently is mainstream childhood a long time ago, I imagine there are viewers inclined to pass over it as sentimental. They might respond similarly to Sambo's occasional custom when we were together in adulthood of giving, apropos of almost nothing, a hushed mock shout: *Yay, Den 2.* In quietly echoing this cheer that closed all of our Cub Scout meetings, he wasn't being schmaltzy; it was a reminder of something we shared that went beyond each of us. He didn't live in the past, but he insisted on the importance of keeping it alive. And while there is deep feeling in his drawing of Den 2, I find nothing sentimental in his making of it. Practicing his drawing skills early in his career, and working on a scale much larger than the original 8x10 inch photo, he recreated the eleven of us with what at first appears to be photographic accuracy. A closer look reveals that the boys arranged around a municipal barbeque grill are pure graphite. Well..., almost pure—for Sambo did something in his drawing that to me was surprising: He blew up the original photograph to the exact scale of the large drawing he wanted to do, then pasted pieces of the photo, collage-like, into his preliminary sketch.

On the figure of the tallest boy, Tommy Ward, standing at one end of the waist-high brick slab, he superimposed Tommy's photographed cap brim, the right shoulder and sleeve of his Cub Scout uniform, and the nylon stretch belt, thought corny by the rest of us, that was handed down from his father. At Tommy's shoulder stands Hunter Horgan— nothing photographed there, except Hunter's shoes, one resting on the edge of the other. Of Billy Wolfe, our heavy-set Den Chief standing at the other end of the bricks, Sambo retained the photographed swelling pockets of his Boy Scout shirt. The four smallest of us sit on the bricks. Al Rose and I are drawn entirely. Tiny Cyle Ferguson is between us, two thirds of his shirt a photographed swatch. And to my right..., Jimmy Grant. Jimmy's loosely clasped hands are pasted in, and his is the only face borrowed from the photograph; it stands out and makes a viewer notice that the rest of our faces are indistinctly sketched and seem prematurely faded. None of us is clearly smiling. The remaining four crouch in the foreground, each with a knee to the earth. Hunter Webb's right arm and hand are pasted from the photo; his left hand trails absently out of sight along his side and into the grass, ever ready I know to pick up a bug. Both of Bobby Castle's photographed hands are in plain view. Less can be seen of rugged Jerry Sims half-kneeling between Bobby and Sambo; Jerry is all drawing except for part of his neckerchief. For himself, Sambo took from the photo only his own left hand and sleeve cuff. The fingers of the hand he drew with, his right, are in the neck fur of a cocker spaniel lying between his knees. This was a neighbor's dog, Rusty. He followed Sambo everywhere. Sambo's rendering of him incorporated nothing from the photograph; it's near perfect and captures the dog's expression.

I sense that in recent years Sambo considered his drawing of Den 2 as not much more than apprentice work. But when he finished it in the1970s, he was pleased enough with the result to hang it in his house, to make copies of it reduced to the size of the original 8x10 inch photograph, and to send one to each of us former scouts. Years later, after he began teaching, he wrote and often said that a sketch knows its truths before the artist/architect does. In reflecting on how the knowledge in his sketch of Den 2 may have guided him through the completed drawing, I notice parallels between this work and his necessarily artistic and documentary career:

In the drawing, he filtered the eleven of us individually through his imagination. At the same time, guiding by the photograph and including parts of it, he made sure that what he produced was informed by actualities a camera can record. The extraordinary extent to which his career integrated dimensions of living and working that often become compartmentalized is now well known. Despite— and as a result of—his sure, gentle manliness, the whole of Sambo's achievement honors the archetypically feminine, and not only because every artist gives birth or because dwellings are naturally embracive. Empathy and human nurture, impulses arguably more common in women than men, are essential to his example in the personal, professional, social, political, environmental, and spiritual dimensions of his life and work. As early as 1993, he spoke of "trying to glimpse the Great Unknown—and trying to render her."[1] His last paintings are dominated by Goddess figures that inspire awe but nullify strife. It's not surprising that one of his last undertakings, the one that he said "will be my great project as an architect," a "jump in the dark... higher and deeper"[2] than all his others, is a pair of "sister houses" for two women, Amy Murphy and Lucy Harris—one living in his native Mississippi, one in his adopted place, Mason's Bend, Alabama; one a person of means, one a single mother without them; one white, one black—and that graduates of the Rural Studio will build Lucy Harris's house. Is it coincidental that

Sambo was close to so many beneficently powerful women: his wife, Jackie; his mother, Margaret; his sister Martha Anne, who extended his life; his grandmother, Sweetee; his daughters, Margaret, Sarah Anne, and Carol? To be sure, there were important men also: his father, whom he called Naumie; his son, Julius; the models he chose to emulate in Meridian, Homer Casteel and Chris Risher. But I'd say the greatest power in the work he did in a still predominantly male profession is fundamentally female; it's power comparable to the way mothers' love is often deeper and more sustaining than even the invaluable contributions of fathers.

I once questioned him about his drawing of Den 2, curious as to why he selected the particular photograph fragments that he did. He wouldn't answer me directly; still, I understood that hands are hard to draw, faces too—that probably explained most of it, and initially I was satisfied to leave it at that. *But what about Jimmy Grant?* I wanted to know later. Jimmy was a nice person; yet none of us who were already close friends as Cub Scouts knew him very well. By the time we reached high school, he was a friendly enough presence, but we thought of him primarily as a likable acquaintance. Whatever else about Jimmy that deserved attention was lost on most of us. *Why Jimmy's face?* I asked him. And why just his? Why not someone else's too? *Hell, Bates...*, he sniffed, regarding me appraisingly, maybe with amusement. The rest he tossed off so casually I almost forgot it: *You never want to give away all your secrets. . . . Do you?* Although he eventually told us, for instance, the secret of how he and Naumie did the Wizard, I doubt that he gave away many of the others, the ones in his work. But, even if he didn't easily let go of his secrets, I expect that subsequent students and admirers of Sambo will continue the discovery of how strongly he imparts them.
— *Randy Bates*

[1] Randolph Bates, "Interview with Samuel Mockbee," *Mockbee Coker: Thought and Processs*. Ed. Lori Ryker. New York: Princeton Architectural Press, 1995. 91-101; 101.
[2] Vernon Mays, "Work in Progress." *Residential* Architect (November - December, 2001). 40-50; 50.

"OBLIQUITY OF THE ECLIPTIC"

The month after Sambo died, as a thesis student, I was asked by the Home and Garden Channel, "What is Samuel Mockbee's legacy?"

I didn't know the answer at the time.

Throughout this year, being called the "clerk of works"*, I have listened to architectural critics, artists, academia, students, photographers, and professionals from around the world, each of them holding a curiosity about the direction, pace, and future of the Rural Studio.

At the end of a long year after:
   29 Wednesday night colloquiums
   an exhibition in Vienna, Austria
   1st annual Newbern Cook-off [ingredients taken only from GB's mercantile store]
   eating fried crab claws at the Red Barn
   completing 4 community projects, 4 Outreach projects, and a house for Musicman
   cooking not just one pig at the annual pig roast, but TWO.
   laying 7000 sq.ft. of sod in the amphitheatre with AJ and Fred [inmates from
       the local state penitentiary]
   visiting New York and the United Nations building, with Julius screaming
       "war eagle" out of the moon roof of the stretch limo
and finally, building an exhibition in Barcelona, Spain.[Sambo would have loved the food]

I now have an answer to the earlier question.

I believe that Sambo's legacy is the continuing spirit of the Rural Studio.

thank you Sambo.

*One of the greatest things about being called "clerk of works" is the chance to drive a Ford/F-350 Superduty utility truck through Hale County. As AJ, Fred, and I drove toward the State Cattle Ranch each evening, we would sometimes get the chance to watch a fiery orange sky as the sun set over the catfish ponds.

Words seem so dangerous, or treacherous. Maybe I should make a drawing for these pages, for a little ambiguity. Hmmm, doesn't look much like Sambo, not really and there is no way I will capture the stunning, subtle beauty of the landscape of Hale County. And Sambo drew so well. OK, forget that. I could borrow one of Stoner's sketches from this year's pig roast in Newbern. They capture the spirit of that incredible place, and of those who gathered there to celebrate Sambo, in a way that I know I can't. Everyone at the pig roast saw the fireworks; fewer probably felt the underlying sadness. Sambo would've loved the fireworks. That outdoor theater was really important to Sambo, and even Chantilly, patched together and partially renovated, looks pretty good. What will others do for this catalog? Sambo knew a lot of smart people, so I know they will all do something really smart, or clever. I've had the chance to write before, and though too generous to really let on, I know Sambo felt as though I'd let him down.

It was always a little scary to speak publicly when he was present. I had the opportunity a number of times, at Sambo's invitation, mostly with students at the Rural Studio. I was always afraid I'd sound pompous, or dull. Or that I'd somehow disappoint him. Sambo spoke so well himself, always the right tone, and confident but not too much so. Milwaukee, a few years ago, speaking to architecture school administrators in conference at the Pfister Hotel: he was the smartest person in the room, though he'd have denied this. There might have been a hundred more rural studios after Sambo spoke that day, in a hun-

dred schools of architecture, if only there were more people like Sambo to go around. I knew Sambo well, though certainly not nearly as well as many others did (their insights will be more insightful than mine will.) He was a friend, though we were not as close as he was with others. We went to a couple World Series games together in Atlanta in 1991, and we had a few beers. I had the privilege of many hours of conversation with him at Auburn, and many more while I served informally as his driver for one academic quarter in Newbern. I think I have some understanding of how he saw the world, and of those things that motivated him to do what he did, but it would be a disservice to him for me to attempt to explain him. I know that he knew that we all have certain obligations, and that we need to figure out what they are. He did, and in Hale County he found the playing field on which to meet them. Van Morrison called it the "inarticulate speech of the heart."

Sambo was approached often by writers working on articles about the Rural Studio, or about him, and he occasionally deflected them toward me. Each time it seemed a little more difficult, a little scarier. "A good human being, with a big heart" I'd nearly always say in those phone conversations. Too much more than that sounded like hype, or seemed invasive. Whatever I said, it never seemed quite sufficient. He was a good human being, with a big heart. It was a privilege to know him.

Most who read this catalog, or who have seen the exhibition to which it is attached, will learn a little about the work of the Auburn Rural Studio, and about Sambo. Some will know a few of the projects through direct experience. Hale County, though, will be Hale County for only a very short time. The suburbs of Tuscaloosa are growing inexorably toward Greensboro and Newbern, bringing progress, envelopment, and building inspectors. One can read into this sprawl the inevitable end of the Rural Studio. Five more years? Ten? Maybe America's suburbs will find their Sambo, too.

I recommend a visit (and soon) to see Hale County and Alabama's Black Belt as Sambo saw them. Stop in to say hello to G.B. at his store in Newbern. Try breakfast at Mustang Oil in Greensboro. Lunch at Dorothy's Country Kitchen outside of Greensboro, though you'll need to look hard or ask around to find it. The Red Barn was often Sambo's choice for dinner, on U.S. 80 in Demopolis. While driving, pop in a compact disc, Dan Bern's Smartie Mine. We listened to this on the drive to Atlanta for the Rural Studio exhibition at the Nexus Gallery. "Sometimes I wish I was Tiger Woods, Tiger Woods…" Sambo loved it.

Sambo was a painter. When we were together, I tried to encourage him to paint more. I'd compare him to Walt Whitman more than to other painters. Just as there is the suggestion of something more heroic than everyday architecture in the "everyday architecture" of the title for this exhibition, there is something heroic and poetic in Sambo's paintings. Whitman; maybe a little Dante.

I know very little about the process that squelched the posthumous awarding of the AIA Gold Medal to Sambo. I have difficulty imagining anyone who deserved it more. This may illustrate that there is greater poverty in the institutional side of the architecture profession than there is in Hale County. There seem to be so many ways, so many excuses, to rationalize not doing what is right. It is sad that this has been done for a person who worked so hard to do what is right, and to do what is good. Maybe it would have been different, maybe he'd have received the medal, if he'd been known as Samuel. Probably too few who voted on this really knew him at all.

People in Mason's Bend knew him. On the morning of one of my trips to the Rural Studio, I heard a report on National Public Radio about the announcement of a Clinton administration initiative on race relations. I didn't pay close attention. That afternoon I was walking with Sambo toward Shepard and Alberta Bryant's house in Mason's Bend. We passed a trailer as one man was arriving home. "Ay, Sambo" he shouted as he turned toward us, smiling. Sambo made a dent in the world.

– David BUEGE

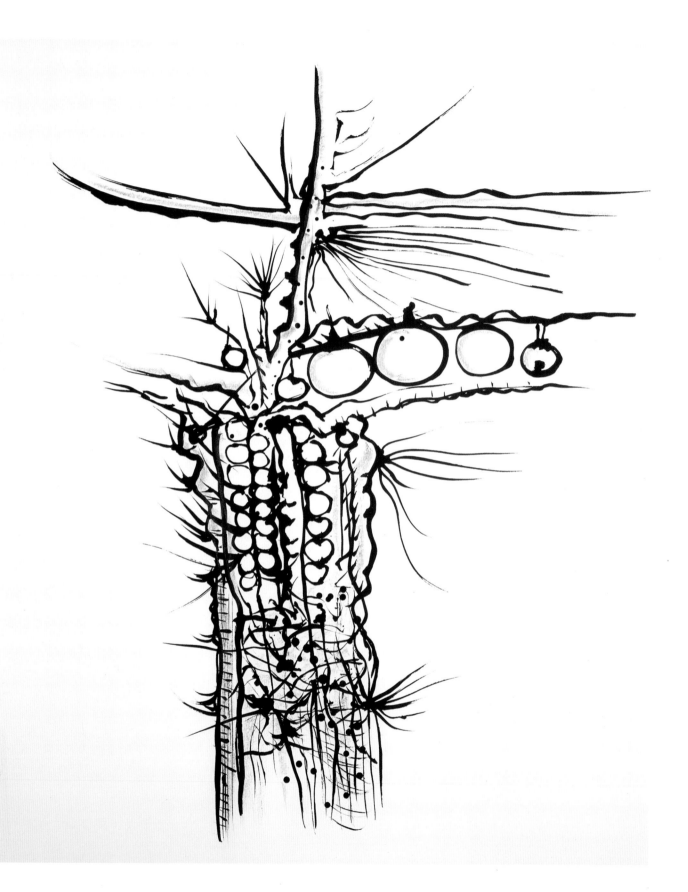

WILLIAM CHRISTENBERRY
[address redacted]
[address redacted]
[phone redacted]
[fax redacted]
[email redacted]

I first met Samuel Mockbee about seven years ago on a hot, humid day in

Newbern, Alabama. Immediately, our conversation took on a good-natured but intense

discussion on the Alabama Crimson Tide and Auburn Tiger football rivalry. (He

supported Auburn, of course, and I, Alabama.) This same discussion would be continued

each and every time we saw one another, before moving to subjects such as the past and

the present situations of the Rural Studio, and my photographs and sculpture.

The accomplishments of the Rural Studio have significant meaning, not only for

Hale County and its people, but also for the whole world. Sambo was a visionary, and his

conscience, integrity and caring for all people and things were always evident to those

who had the privilege of knowing him.

In May, 2001, my father had just passed away in Tuscaloosa. Sambo, friends and I

had lunch at his favorite bar-b-que joint. He asked if he could come by my parents' house

to pay his respects to my mother. As he left the house, I walked him to his pickup truck.

We began to discuss ideas for projects we might pursue together in the future. It was

exciting conversation. As he was about to get in his truck, I noticed a live turtle resting in

the bed of the pickup. Sambo had rescued it a few hours earlier from the middle of a Hale

County red earth road.

SAMBO MOCKBEE's achievements as an architect, artist and educator are well-established and enormous.

The contributions he made to my personal journey as an architect and as an individual are immeasurable.

In 1993, I was first introduced to Sambo as a second-year student at Auburn. I was selected with nine other students to attend the Rural Studio and help complete Shepard and Alberta Bryants' remarkable Hay Bale House. It was during this exciting quarter of study that I began to understand what the title of architect actually means and to fully appreciate the responsibilities carried with it.

Sambo's process was straightforward. He introduced our student group to the Bryants, the Hay Bale House and surrounding Hale County, then simply turned us loose. There was no classroom detachment or abstract theory on this project. My fellow students and I were face-to-face with real people, real needs, and real life.

Sambo intuited that each of us was prepared to step up to the plate and take moral responsibility for our actions. The elements we drew on paper and constructed with our own hands had to work…by that I mean they had to fulfill the practical needs of our clients. At the same time, the result had to be beautiful and posses that glimmer of "stamango" (what Sambo referred to as the ethereal quality of architecture which elevates a structure to an aesthetic presence far beyond four walls and a roof).

I quickly learned that Sambo employed teaching methods that were his alone. He would simply point out a problem and quietly step away, shifting the responsibility for a suitable solution to us. Rather than condescend to his students, he treated us as fully-capable equals!

In retrospect, the best lesson I learned from Sambo was to trust my inner voice—my muse as he called it—and not second-guess gut instinct. The self-confidence instilled by Sambo enabled us to evolve as thinkers, designers and human beings. We departed from Hale County a short twelve weeks later, but we took with us knowledge and wisdom that would last a lifetime.

I spent the next two years missing Sambo, Hale County and everything that both had given me. I missed the MAGIC!

Happily, I returned to Hale County in 1996 with thesis partner Iain Stewart to begin work on the Goat House, our design-build thesis project. Once again, Sambo guided us with a silent, steady hand. He stopped by once or twice a week to review our progress, never telling us, "Don't do this" or "You'd better do that." Sambo expertly reviewed our models and drawings, gently reminding us to acknowledge our time constraints and assess the amount of work we could actually accomplish by the end of the school year.

Of course, like any savvy mentor, Sambo occasionally used methods that were more…direct. I remember one critique in which he chatted with us while playing idly with a large, decorative piece on our model of the Goat House. The piece suddenly broke off into his hand with a small snap, and Sambo apologized briefly before climbing into his little Diahatsu and telling us, "Proceed and be bold." It wasn't until later that we realized this was Sambo's way of challenging us to step back and rethink a design excess.

Proceed and be bold. This was Sambo's signature admonition to his students, and the words will remain with me forever. They are simple to say, but often very difficult to live up to. Sambo Mockbee, my mentor and friend, obviously discovered the means to do just that.

The time I spent with Sambo and the Rural Studio was one of the most important experiences in my education as an architect. While Sambo's art and architecture are creations that can be viewed, critiqued, and admired, an equally-important legacy will be the tremendous inspiration he provided to the eager, young minds influenced by his unique approach to teaching—and life.

Josh C. Cooper
Auburn University - 1997

capable equals.

In retrospect, the best lesson I learned from Sambo was to trust my inner voice—my muse as he called it—and not second-guess gut instinct. The self-confidence instilled by Sambo enabled us to evolve as thinkers, designers and human beings. We departed from Hale County a short twelve weeks later, but we took with us knowledge and wisdom that would last a lifetime.

I spent the next two years

------Original Message------
From: andrea dean ███████████████████
Sent: Monday, June 09, 2003 7:58 AM
To: ████████████████
Subject: essay on Sambo Mockbee

About Sambo by Andrea Oppenheimer Dean

In late Spring of 2000, shortly after Samuel "Sambo" Mockbee became the first architect to win a MacArthur "genius" grant, I called to interview him for an article in *Architectural Record*. I'd admired his work for years, but I'd never met him and was curious. I knew him to be an inspired designer and a charismatic teacher and soon learned that he also was a painter, a poet, an environmentalist, and a humanist who acted on his convictions. I especially liked the fact that during the heady 1990s, when many well-known architects ignored social and civic challenges to concentrate on extravagant buildings for wealthy clients around the world, Mockbee chose to focus on serving poor black clients near his home in the rural South. In his private practice he had created formally powerful work, but his proudest and most lasting contribution was the Rural Studio, which he founded in 1992 and directed until his death in 2001. There, he and his students designed and built modest, innovative, "warm, dry, and noble" buildings, as he put it, for people who simply needed decent shelter.

In that first interview, Mockbee's civility, modesty, and fire came through. He said that running the Rural Studio was "like packing up and going to war." He was referring, in part, to his 170-mile drive every Monday morning from his home and family in Canton, Mississippi, to the Alabama hamlet of Newbern, the Rural Studio's home. There he lived during the week in a drafty farmhouse and taught mostly white, Southern, and middle-class architecture students how to design and build for poor African-Americans. He also led seminars on the social and ethical responsibilities of architects, was fundraiser-in-chief for the Rural Studio, and lectured about it at universities nationwide.

cont. ⟶

At the end of our telephone conversation, Mockbee asked what big project I was working on. Without missing a beat, I said I'd love to write a book about him and the Rural Studio. And so began the thread that lead to *Rural Studio: Samuel Mockbee and an Architecture of Decency* (Princeton Architectural Press, 2002).

During my visits to Newbern, I learned that the Rural Studio represented a vision of architecture that embraced hands-on architectural education, social welfare, the use of unusual building materials, recycling, sustainability, and an aesthetics of place.

Mockbee founded the studio as a sort of junior year abroad for Auburn University architecture students, but instead of locating the studio in a foreign country he chose one of America's poorest counties, Hale. Walker Evans and James Agee visited this place during the Great Depression and in their book *Let Us Now Praise Famous Men* memorialized Hale's white sharecroppers. Most of the Rural Studio's clients, however, are African-Americans, "left behind by Reconstruction," in Mockbee's way of thinking. Although the Rural Studio has peppered Hale County with a growing collection of new houses and community buildings, the towns and countryside still look eerily unchanged from the place evoked by Evans and Agee.

Mockbee treated the Rural Studio's clients with respect and affection, an example his students naturally followed. He made sure the studio's designs were tailored to the clients' needs and wishes, not to a designer's whim. When creating a house for Shepard and Alberta Bryant of Mason's Bend, for instance, the students first showed the elderly couple a scheme for a two-story house set back from the dusty road. The Bryants' acceptance was qualified: they wanted their home set close to the road so folks could see it, they said, and they wanted a one-story. The students obliged.

Teaching methods at the Rural Studio replaced the usual contemplation of theory and "paper architecture" exercises with hands-on design and construction and nose-to-nose negotiations with real clients. For many students, it was their first intimate brush with poverty, and the experiences inspired what Mockbee called "a moral sense of service to the community."

In part because he wanted to build inexpensively, Mockbee taught his students to use recycled and curious materials—hay bales, concrete rubble, colored bottles, cast-off automobile tires, car windshields, outdated license plates, road signs, baled cardboard waste. To form the walls of the so-called tire chapel, they filled a thousand donated used tires with soil, fortified then with reinforcing bars, wrapped them with wire mesh, and coated them with stucco. They used a stash of cast-off car windshields to make a glazed roof for the community center in Mason's Bend. And they built a students' living quarters out of waste, baled corrugated cardboard. The studio transmuted ordinary materials into extraordinary objects.

Not surprisingly, the studio's buildings bear a strong affinity to Mockbee's designs for private clients. Like his Barton House in Madison County, Miss., and his Cook House in Oxford, Miss., the studio's work is contemporary modernism grounded in Southern culture. It has a decidedly quirky touch.

One Rural Studio student told me Mockbee presented himself as a "cross between a Mississippi redneck and an art freak." Certainly, Mockbee was passionate about his art and his architecture. But his students seemed most deeply touched by his humanity and his moral compass. They told me about his admonition that as architects their goodness and compassion counted more than their passion or greatness. I met students galvanized not only by Mockbee's brilliant designs but also by his bone-deep decency and belief in the worth of the individual. In the Socratic tradition of teaching through self-knowledge, he let students make their own mistakes and find their own solutions. They, in turn, identified closely with a teacher who took them into a landscape they'd not previously experienced, a place close to them in miles but distant in social terms.

A comment Mockbee made about Shepard Bryant stays with me. Bryant is a fisherman who lived in an unheated shack without plumbing until the Rural Studio built a house for him and his family. Mockbee described Bryant as "a gentle man who'd had a hard time but wasn't bitter or mad about anything." I asked the architect, a very gentle man himself, whether that wasn't true of him also. I was thinking mainly about his battle with leukemia, which he didn't try to conceal. Mockbee didn't say he identified with Bryant. What he said was, "I looked the death merchant in the face and laughed at him." He told me he wanted to leave behind "something that's going to have power and live long after my living personality is gone. I've got to keep pushing so that what I leave is as significant as I can make it. I'm getting close," he said, "but I'm not there." That was late in 2001, shortly before his death that December.

He did leave behind something that appears to be organically intact and vigorous. I've had occasion to return to the Rural Studio a couple of times since he died. There are five completed new projects, including the last one initiated by Sambo, a house with walls made of waste carpet tiles for a woman named Lucy Harris, plus a storefront, a church, a pavilion in a park, and a community center. More buildings are under construction. Andrew Freear, formerly Sambo's right hand and now the studio's co-director, shepherded most of the new projects, and two or three are quite exceptional. The recent work is different from what came before, as different as Freear is from his mentor. That's all to the good. The Rural Studio changed constantly during the founder's brief tenure, and it remains a work in progress. But Samuel Mockbee's convictions and energy endure.

To his credit, the Rural Studio thrives.

SAMUEL MOCKBEE AS MASTER KNOT OF FATE

PAULA DEITZ

In October 1998, I met Samuel Mockbee at Smith College during a symposium I co-organized called "Speaking of Architecture: A World View." He had only recently learned of his leukemia but came anyway with his customary gusto intact. The day turned out to be a celebration of humanism in architecture, and the lives of three hundred students and alumnae were transformed forever because of his courage in not allowing his illness to alter the course of his life. We watched the elegant, functional and sustainable architecture of the Rural Studio unfold on the screen, and he spoke movingly of discovering the Mississippi gravesite of James Chaney, one of the three civil rights workers murdered in the summer of 1964. This accidental proximity to courage transformed Sambo's own life.

Interspersed among the slides were his paintings, a phantasmagoria of images in deeply glowing colors, and we understood how important to his creative imagination was this integration of art and architecture. For him, the initial influence for making architecture was "the emotion of art rather than a concept," as he put it. Above all, his paintings, collages and prints, revealed in cinematic progression, told the story of a personal mythology that intertwined and glorified the people and places he knew along the Black Warrior River in the economically impoverished communities of rural Alabama.

Later, after one of his subsequent visits to New York, I received in the mail an etching and a photograph from Sambo with the following description: "The enclosed

MASTER KNOT OF FAITH

The Black Warrior drifts
Bound by a Master Knot of Fate
Floating among the graves of the abused
Drifting past the dreams of the neglected
Embracing an eddy of a Butterfly's psyche
Flooding a delta of Goodness, Happiness and Good Fortune

The Black Warrior drifts
Its ancient liquid light walking on water
To the Horizon Line where angels like to drink before
Evaporating toward a summit unknown and
Returning with earth-bound eggs and spirit-bound sperm
Deep in the Heart of Dixie.

—SAMUEL MOCKBEE

Shepherd Bryant with grandsons and decapitated loggerhead turtle, Mason's Bend, Hale County, Alabama. Photographer: Timothy Hursley.

etching is part of the evolving rural mythology that I have been exploring over the years. The turtle is representative of Shepherd Bryant, and the young pagan goddess is his granddaughter, Apple. . . . The enclosed photograph of Shepherd Bryant and his grandsons was taken at "Mason's Bend" about four years ago. I thought you might find it interesting, if not beautiful in both a primeval and contemporary sense."

Therein lies the beginning of the tale of the etching *Master Knot of Fate*. Because I felt it bore clues to Sambo's view of the world, I brought it with me to show while I spoke at the memorial program for him at the Max Protetch Gallery in March 2002. Upon seeing it that day, his youngest daughter Carol, who had assisted her father in printing the etching in 1998, told me that it was the only one in the edition that he had filled in with watercolor. Her information combined with Sambo's own explication provided the impetus to study this iconic etching in greater depth.

Even people who have not yet visited the Rural Studio have come to know families like the Bryants of Mason's Bend through photographs and videos of their lives and of their soaring and quirky houses and local community center, all constructed with imaginative recycled materials. The Bryants' 1994 Hay Bale House—with its full-width columned front porch sheltered under the light airiness of a corrugated acrylic roof—was the first to be completed by Rural Studio students, proving what Sambo called the power of architecture to change lives and solidify communities.

Not a young man, Bryant catches loggerhead turtles in the Black Warrior River for food and hauls them up to the house, some weighing as much as seventy pounds. Like a trophy of the hunt, he painted one of the shells a bright blue and displayed it on the porch where it matched the base trim of the yellow columns. The photograph of him with his three grandsons and the decapitated turtle by Timothy Hursley has come to be recognized as a small masterpiece.

In *The Mythic Image*, when Joseph Campbell describes the imagery of the world mountain in a sculpted relief on a twelfth-century B.C. Babylonian boundary stone, he passes through the upper stages to the watery abyss below, where dwell the mythological prototypes of the classical four elements. There, the tortoise, representing water itself, supports the entire cosmic mountain with his feet. In a sense, Sambo

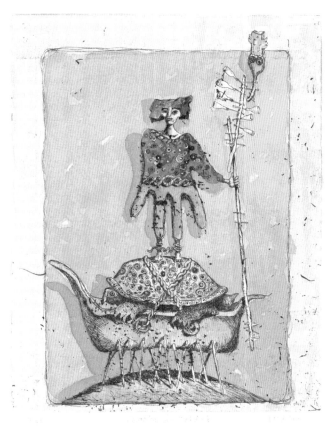

MASTER KNOT OF FATE, *by Samuel Mockbee, 1997. Etching with watercolor, numbered 16/80, 18 ⅞ x 14 ¾ inches.*

reversed this imagery in his recurring private mythology in which the turtle, the steadfast patriarchal figure of Shepherd Bryant, tied to a tublike boat, is propelled across the world on myriad legs of sharp beaver sticks.

Held aloft as the pagan goddess is Apple—granddaughter actually of a rural Mississippi matriarch though linked in Sambo's mythology to Bryant—here in the guise of the "hand woman" with the middle two fingers of her lower extremities metamorphosed back into feet. She is the hand of fate and of fortune holding firmly in her one real hand a staff that is the quintessential bottle tree, whose bare limbs are covered with antique bottles that suck up evil spirits. Topping this ensemble is one of Sambo's beloved and slightly animistic yellow gourds.

Enriched by the background glow of an orange sunset, the world here is green as is the mottled shell of the turtle and its distinctive beaked head. The bright eyelike points of color on the shell are repeated in primary hues on the goddess's garment whose bright blue background recalls her grandfather's trophy tortoise shell.

Though, like the turtle bound to his boat, the goddess's feet are tied together with rope—and a rope design encircles her neck and waist—the implication is not that freedom is prohibited but that we are tied to our fate and to each other, as Sambo's friends have discovered following his death. He became the Master Knot of Fate; and in the poem that accompanies the etching, he saw the flow of the Black Warrior River ultimately as a source of renewal.

PAULA DEITZ *is Editor of* THE HUDSON REVIEW *in New York.*

Some Observations on the Art of Samuel Mockbee

When referring to the formidable task of writing the text for *Let Us Now Praise Famous Men*, James Agee writes in a letter to Father Flye in August 1938:

My trouble is, such a subject cannot be seriously looked at without intensifying itself toward a centre which is beyond what I, or anyone else, is capable of writing of; the whole problem and nature of existence.

There is a special portion of the population of Hale County, Alabama, who became the clients of the now well-known Rural Studio, a program extension of the College of Architecture at Auburn University. I doubt anyone else had the complex relationship and experience that Samuel Mockee (Sambo) had with his clients in Hale County, a place that could be characterized externally as intimate, yet culturally divided by class and race. For Sambo, it was an experience filled with conflict and personal struggle, yet teaming with joy and the privilege of providing his clients with shelter and place.

Through these relationships, there grew an impressive body of architecture that has attracted much celebration from down low to very high regions of praise. Mockbee's innovative campaigns in architecture and teaching bled freely into a profound and complex body of paintings and works on paper. His dedication to self-expression, experimentation, and celebration coalesced into a magnificent, challenging artistic form.

Patrons of these works describe them as mystical and mythical, terms that hint at a high-spirited process. After closely viewing a few large-scale pieces from the late 1990s, and some of his sketches, I would add that his paintings are complicated, metaphorical, personal environments that contain yet-to-be-told truths about our humanity and about their creator. The opportunity to view his artwork is a chance to get a close look at a man who reached out to his culture and surroundings (with much enthusiasm and joy), giving it his all and asking for nothing in return.

The Ascension of Shephard Bryant, 1999, Oil on plywood in painted plywood frame, 96 x 48 inches

His pictorial, expressive approach to painting is partially informed by an observation of his subject. Although there is an animated, totemic assemblage that serves to narrate Mockbee's work, his keen visual sensibilities document, with careful rendering, his clients' characters and living traditions. He adds a gentle judgment or a moral-to-the-story quality to his work. *The Ascension of Shepard Bryant* demonstrates this with its central image of a large turtle, suspended by its left hind foot by rope strung to a tree and fastened at its base. Rope is wrapped in a fashion used for limb lowering (coiled around the trunk several times). His turtle's chisel-sharp mouth references the earth, a plumb point. Pinned in the coiled rope is a haunting solitary figure (Mr. Bryant). He is labeled like a store-front with a T-shirt that reads "Bait Shop." Sambo has depicted him enslaved in his own desires and occupation as a fisherman of the Black Warrior River, reminding us of the entrapment we all experience in our own lives.

A swallowtail butterfly is poised on the back of the turtle, perhaps a reference to the Butterfly House located at Mason's Bend. Mockbee treated the painted atmosphere so as to render it as twilight or water. Standing guard before the figure is an attentive rooster, blending into the plane with gray-blue monochromatic tones. Color reverses the function of this rooster, a bird of fashion, fury, and flame. Above in the upper corner, another set of yard birds is perched high in a tree for nocturnal rest. They face each other in silhouette; together they depict the head of a man, one of many references to opposing forces, a man, divided, literally. This might reflect Sambo's divided existence between his world and the world of his Black Belt clients.

Mockbee's actively painted surfaces serve as a record of evolving form. There is some evidence in the work's painted skin that points to the possibility that he created this work outside the traditional studio setting. The lower right-hand region has a sandy surface, perhaps the result of his brush's contact with clay, sand, or dirt located at the base of the painting. Sambo's working method was nontraditional (by contemporary standards) in that he preferred working outdoors, in the surreal, southern heat. His studio was an assembly of cedar poles that held a huge tarpaulin. Mockbee liked natural lighting for viewing his paintings. His work area was filled with a variety of painting gizmos that helped him reach up high or make a certain sort of stroke.

Mockbee's treatment of detail, form, and spaces reflect their assembly process. He makes no attempt to engage a seamless, painted simulation. Rather, parts that comprise the whole are clearly in evidence, even celebrated. In his paintings, there is a sharp division between his amorphous background and an intensely embellished subject. This spatial treatment reminds me of the drive along the two-lane back roads Mockbee made between the various project sites. The lush green fields blurring by act as a sedative, adding to the feeling of being detached from reality, and connect the traveler/outsider to the acute human conditions found at each site.

Mockbee undertook a departure from a straightforward approach to painting in a number of large pieces. With a playful attitude, he embraced all that was possible for appropriation into his own process. For example, he employed Robert Rauschenberg's painting construction methods. Sambo attached everything from tire treads to beaver sticks (sacred to him), to painted gourds and beautifully integrated them compositionally. In the painting entitled *Apple*, the central character's gaze is oddly seductive (this effect is present in many other pieces). Beautifully rendered feet hold one's attention for a moment before the brilliantly painted surfaces lead the viewer elsewhere. Mockbee used great care in building the woman's feet, which was somewhat like washing them. Rich clay red/orange hues contrast with brilliant evergreens that, together, are visually seductive. Through the painting, viewers find themselves in Eden and this may be Eve (sex) who has captured the senses. Sambo imposed his sense of the divided in this piece by introducing a more demonic second Eve (death) image that

is literally an attachment hanging on a thread (actually from coiled wire and nail). He treated this second head more crudely yet with invention. It is fabricated plywood, cut into with a saw, collaged with roofing felt and a single red feather.

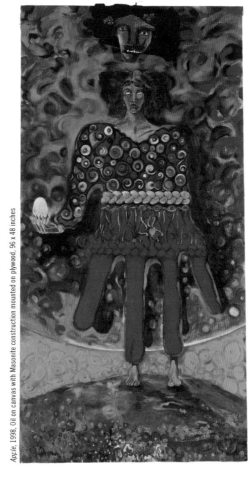

Apple, 1998, Oil on canvas with Masonite construction mounted on plywood, 96 x 48 inches

There is much to gain from examining Mockbee's sketches due to the fact that they often contain great clarity and are unaltered. Painting naturally offers the option of burying an image within its layers. One such piece is *Tupac, One Love, Mason's Bend, Alabama* (2001, pen, pencil, ink, gouache, and photo collage on paper, 18 x 24 inches). It is an amalgam of what could be found at Mason's Bend, where there are at least

four building projects in place. Mockbee was excited that this work contained a color photo collage image of the blown-out red (early '70s) Ford Pinto that was in the yard up on blocks, a predictable find in this harsh, southern landscape. Someone had written into the dust on the hatchback window "Tupac One Love lives." This thrilled Sambo to no end that Tupac (and his tragic death), could reach to this remote culture, blurring time and place, and melding into the rural mythology. A skull-headed beast (which appears in other late pieces) stands over Shepard and Alberta Bryant, perhaps as a death presence. This invented form also reflects Mockbee's belief in some ancient presence or afterlife being that has survived in the Alabama Black Belt area to accompany its ongoing dark, oppressive history. Mockbee was fond of asking his students when looking at their projects, "OK, Where's the sex and death? — key ingredients for good design.

Another drawing entitled *The Bus @ Mason's Bend: The Raft of the Black Warrior* (1997, ink, marker, and colored pencil on paper, 15 x 18 inches) reflects a combination of thumbnail sketches. The central image is a converted yellow school bus, a well-known feature in Mason's Bend, located in a meandering, silver-drawn ring that imitates the path of the Black Warrior River. Four handwritten versions of his poem entitled *The Black Warrior* dominate the drawing; the clearest reads as follows:

Bound and tied deep in the Heart of Dixie
The Black Warrior drifts his ancient liquid
light floating toward the unknown.
Hands tied by a Master knot of fate
Drifting among the dreams of the neglected
floating among the graves of the abused
Dreaming...
He passes through a Butterfly's psyche
coming to our rescue
walking on water.

– Bill Dooley

Learning in Newbern

"For it is the character of a seasoned provincial life that it is realistic, or successfully adapted to its natural environment, and that as a consequence it is stable, or hereditable. But it is the character of our urbanized, anti-provincial, progressive, and mobile American life that it is in a condition of eternal flux. Affections, and long memories, attach to the ancient bowers of life in the provinces; but they will not attach to what is always changing."

John Crowe Ransom, I'll Take My Stand

The Rural Studio is acclaimed for the projects of its first decade, which are appreciated as the fruit of virtuous methods: pursuing an ethical practice of architecture, providing assistance to disadvantaged communities, and exploring building methods that foster responsible resource use. But the Rural Studio was not born whole, and has followed the crooked path of youth. The messy reality of architecture students building their designs for local communities compromises as many intentions as it resolves. Critics question the willful quality of student designs, wondering if these are appropriate to the needs of the "needy." The practices of the Rural Studio are not as ecologically sustainable as many wish, the social reforms it has supported fall short of justice, and the craft of its constructions is less than professional. Given its real capacities, the Rural Studio struggles against such standards because learning by doing engages its students and teachers with community members in complex endeavors often beyond their abilities. Does the Rural Studio really work?

That question usually addresses the who, what and why of the Rural Studio, but its location is more telling. It found a place—in the education system, in the profession of architecture, and even on earth, that is profoundly peripheral. The choice by Sambo Mockbee and D. K. Ruth to establish this learning community in Hale County was motivated by a desire to pursue opportunities unavailable on campus and in centers of architectural practice. The removal of the Rural Studio from both the university and the city provides its students and teachers great freedom—from supervision and regulation, and also from distraction. Its isolation allows an experiment where alternative practices are not only researched, but applied, and where belonging to a community encourages students to reflect on what is central to a life of good practice—for a citizen as well as an architect.

In a way its location was a defiant choice, identifying opportunity where most see only problems and pathology. The Black Belt is physically beautiful, but by most social science measures it is failing. Hale County lost half its population from 1900 to 1980, while that of Alabama doubled, and that of the nation nearly tripled. In the 19th century growing cotton here made a few rich, but depended upon the exploitation of the land and its workers—first black slaves, but later white tenants as well, yeomen who moved from subsistence farming in the hills to cotton cropping on the prairies as the antebellum plantation system collapsed. The continuing globalization of textile production forced the abandonment of the cotton economy in West Alabama and the migration of agricultural workers to cities and their factories.

Soil, climate, and history marked this place with a difficult legacy, which well serves the Studio's educational program. Students study the vernacular patterns of the Black Belt, finding remnants of local homesteads among the pastures, woodlands, and catfish farms of what is an increasingly industrialized landscape supplying a narrow range of resources for outside demand. Row crops and subsistence farms are rare, demonstrating how economic progress—in the forms of centralization, the division of labor and distribution of resources—governs not only our work, but where and how we live.

The landscape offers a particularly stark lesson in its legible confrontation between that industrial order and the agrarian one that preceded it. This division has been a source of political and sectional conflict since the founding of the United States, contributing directly to the American Civil War. While rural values lie at the foundation of regional identity in the South, national attitudes favoring self-reliant, small landowners extend beyond any section. Arguments against centralization and bigness, and support for social, political and physical patterns based on independent holdings—the family farm— have particular significance for our nation's designed environment. The continuing impact of agrarian thought on our land and building is evident both in Jefferson's ubiquitous national grid and Frank Lloyd Wright's Broadacre City proposal for a continental landscape of small homesteads.

As an architectural program of the American South, the Rural Studio has been influenced both by traditional critiques of industrialism, and by more recent objections to the implications of market economics like those voiced by the Kentuckian Wendell Berry, who in calling for "an authentic settlement and inhabitation of our country" argues that the industrial economy is fundamentally colonial, based "on the assumption that it is permissible to ruin one place or culture for the sake of another." The Black Belt is filled with the kind of ruined places Berry refers to, and its fallen state provides the Rural Studio the ground necessary to motivate and test an architecture of reform. Region, landscape, and political and architectural tradition all frame the ethos of the Rural Studio in a broadly agrarian context—less for its rural situation, than for its commitment to helping local communities and people be native to their place.

In that commitment, the Rural Studio contradicts assumptions of both the university and the design professions, which reflect the primacy of industrial models in education and commerce today. While the profession of architec-

All bottom photos by Cynthia Connolly

ture is increasingly driven by contract and documentation structures necessary to manage relationships across the extended hierarchy of the building process, the Rural Studio relies on a flat organization where designers do their own building. And where the academy is dominated by abstract research in the laboratory, the Rural Studio extends land grant university outreach to its limits through a unique service-learning model led by undergraduate fieldwork.

These contrasts with predominant method suggest an implicit critique of orthodox professional and academic practice. Where the university and profession establish standing and expertise through methods that distinguish and distance their knowledge from the world, the Rural Studio tends to local projects, learning and applying the homely lessons of custom and experience. Students work in communities where skills are shared, expertise is won in doing, and standing achieved by word-of-mouth.

This grounding of Rural Studio method in place not only allows, but demands an examination of first principles, establishing an exemplary situation in which to begin making architecture. Building is framed as an elemental act, so that student constructions tend to a kind of fundamentalism: big roofs, sheds, basic shelters, and simple foundations. Expressive opportunities are discovered and enrich every episode of building, as for once the process and material of construction are completely familiar to the student. Limited means and skills encourage inventiveness and an opportunistic attitude towards constraint, emphasizing the value of specificity and craft.

Simplicity of means, and dependence on local methods, support and good will encourage the intimacy with one's work that characterizes agrarian life. Instead of encountering sites, clients and building as abstractions, students in Newbern grapple with all directly, and are most often humbled in the confrontation. Their situation encourages students to value loyalty and trust over contract; the dignity of working across the whole over the efficiency of

dividing labor by task; human contact and community over anonymity and system; and reliance on local things rather than on the products of a factory or the expertise of the city.

The primary lessons taught by the Rural Studio are thus agrarian ones: that place matters, that imagining and making enjoy their fullest power only when intimately linked, that good work depends on the practice of responsibility that exists only when the worker feels a stake in and affection for the work.

A dictum ascribed to Thomas Jefferson, that "design activity and political thought are indivisible", summarizes a motivating idea of the Rural Studio. As Sambo Mockbee stated, "what we are trying to create is the citizen architect." Living in the Black Belt, and in Newbern, makes the potentials and responsibilities of architecture and citizenship more plain—these are places to learn the meaning and value of good work.

In fostering that lesson, however, the Rural Studio only plants a seed. Students return to campus and the design studio, and graduate to pursue careers in cosmopolitan centers. Professional qualification requires three years of internship in established architectural practices, followed by licensure through examination. Those experiences enmesh young architects in procedures and habits unfamiliar in Newbern.

The first alumni of the Rural Studio are beginning to establish independent practices, only now walking the new land of their adult lives. Ten years on, their work will make plain whether the lessons of affection and place taught in Newbern are remembered in those practices. Only then will we know if the Rural Studio truly works.

– *John Forney*

"While I have not seen a Sam Mockbee building in person, I've been intrigued with his work since it first surfaced in the architectural publications, and I was fortunate to meet him a couple of times.

I can't say I really knew him, but the work resonated for me, especially in the character of its intent. In my early career, I had some of the same feelings, but they ended up playing out in a different way. I was intrigued enough with him and his work to recommend him to several clients, and we were in the process of making those connections when he passed away. I believe that I missed a great opportunity to know somebody of very special stature and very special talents whose voice has been stilled by fate. I only hope that the trajectory of his thinking has been transferred to a range of younger people who experienced him as a teacher, and that they will take the banner and continue what he started to do. This is a work of honesty, directness and proves that great architecture doesn't require extraordinary budgets, it just requires extraordinary clients who believe in you and whose intentions are honorable. An architect like Sam Mockbee has shown the way for young talents to make a significant contribution in an area of building that is not normally assigned to talented architects. So, I'm sorry for our loss. I am hopeful for the future of Sam's thinking to be realized everywhere, and I'm grateful that he was able to contribute as he did." – *Frank Gehry, Architect*

WHEN SAM MOCKBEE DIED, SOMEWHERE DOWN SOUTH A TREE FELL —

big as an oak, a 57-year marvel in its own place, it drew sustenance from generations of loam and deep water, weathered storms and bent and grew broad, threw off shade and color for all that came and sat beneath it, sheltered all comers, an elemental force that rained out new growth, and, on December 30, returned to its own soil.

If art is seeing and making, to an uncommon degree Sam Mockbee had the soul of an artist. Although a gifted tale-teller, Sambo's métier was not the written word, the usual currency of his region, but graphic and plastic expression. "You know, what I really love to do is make prints," he confessed in a honeyed drawl from a porch swing more than 20 years ago, after hearing Mississippi writers Shelby Foote and Ellen Gilchrist read from their own work. In the studio, this bearded, Richardsonian man lightly skimmed over a drawing board in a far corner of the room, apparently burning with his art, perpetually encircled by a haze of smoke from colored pencils and spray paint and student breath; then the drawings would emerge from a messy pile of tracing paper and blow the room clean.

His elemental love of making art, of looking fearlessly and closely at his own world, translated over time into three-dimensional architecture for people. His houses for the affluent, fiercely unsentimental and rooted in contemporary culture, were complex, unfashionable, personal interpretations that drew inspiration from vernacular traditions—including galvanized roofs, rusting metal scraps, dogtrot forms, porches—and recast them into jazz. Sambo found his voice and made the South sing again. With that same level gaze, this iconoclast, a humorous, self-described "subversive" who was "going to war," saw injustice. Down the back roads of his native region lay shacks with plastic sheeting for doorways, where a reluctant hand would draw the curtain, hiding its private troubles from passersby. Consistently, unapologetically, Sambo raised the curtain and went inside. Although he had grown up in segregated Meridian, Mississippi, just an hour from the earthen dam that once held the bodies of civil rights martyrs, Mockbee came of age later in the army, where he confronted a richer, more racially multidimensional world: His art and his architecture had discovered their subject. Early on, his work stood apart. In the late 1970s, his practice in Jackson, Mississippi, included formally powerful, simple churches and residences. After winning a Progressive Architecture Award for a series of small houses for the rural poor in Madison County, Mississippi, where he lived with his own family, he eventually founded Auburn University's Rural Studio with D.K. Ruth. Based in part on Clemson University's semester in Genoa, Italy, Mockbee improbably reinvented the semester abroad for Hale County, Alabama, a land drenched in sunlight and greenness and rich soil but blighted by persistent poverty.

Sambo's "Redneck Taliesin" raised the temperature in the humid little town and attracted the students. The Rural Studio, which soon garnered international attention, required total engagement of student and teacher (including residency, first in a Faulknerian mansion in Greensboro, later at a farmhouse in Newbern). In a way their mothers never could have imagined, students cooked and cleaned; studied regional architectural history; drew; read literature's great voices; played music; sat up late; met the townspeople; and, especially, planned and built buildings with their hands. Unusual materials (abandoned tires, shards of concrete, hay bales, and rejected windshields) helped provide uncommon personality and presence for the small structures they made, including houses, chapels, and community centers. Simultaneously, the phenomenon multiplied throughout the country, the Rural Studio flourished, and Mockbee's legend swelled.

In lectures, Mockbee frequently quoted Alberti's dictum that we must choose between "fortune and virtue." Sam Mockbee chose virtue, not as judgmental prissiness, but in a robust, compassionate sense of knocking on doors, finding need, and answering it. By engaging students with authentic clients in Alabama communities, he tapped into the natural optimism of the young, freeing them from the more insular, abstract cynicism and formal obsessions of the design studio. A generation of students, now some 400 strong, inspired by the Rural Studio's social activism, has followed in Mockbee's prodigious wake. His real accomplishment, his real art, may lie outside his artful buildings, in the potential work and lives of those that follow, nurtured and liberated and heading out to build. Who among them might take his place?

Re-Memory. by Bruce Lanier

I Took A Wrong Turn In Newbern.
The Old House With Peeling Wallpaper.
A Trip To The Post Office.
Mustang Oil.
Althea.
My "Pigsty."
A $700 Broken Spindle.
Painting The Big House White.
Scaffolding Nearly Tipping Over.
Ed's Hat, Patrick's New Wife.
Slideshows.
Football In The Front Yard.
CK Balloons.
Sambo's Naps.
The Short Bus.
Clawfoot Fried Chicken.
Green Bunny.
House Tours.
Cutting Slate.
Dirtman's Wedding.
This isn't NASA, Man.
The Girl From The Pig.
Velvet.
Moving Out Of The Big House.
You Can Work For Somebody Better Than That.
We Need To Get You Working For An Architect.
You'll Make A Great Architect. You Procrastinate.
Clinton, AL.
The Night Before New York.
Talking To Blue Men.
Epic Drinking At McSorley's.
Subversive.
Tate's My Boy.
Meet Thom Mayne.
Wanda's Toast, Sambo's Recovery.
Steven Holl.
Skipping Out To Wait For Harper.
Sambo In Auburn.
Evenings At Amsterdam.
Drinking Games.
Can You Name All 50 States In 5 Minutes?
Where Does Sambo Live?
It's A Death Camp.
Surprise--The First Visit To Japonica Path.
The Grasshopper Response.
Jack's Paper.
Garbage On A Tarp.
Kegerator, Chickens, And A Goat.
Hide And Go Seek.
You Guys Think You Have More Time Than You Do.
Slip And Slide.
Pulling Down The Porch.
A Busted Nose.
Mrs. Francis' Eggs and Bacon.
El Paso.
Ring Of Fire.
Take It Easy, Sunglasses, and Four Movies.
Fast Orange In My Hair.
20 Stolen Dollars.
Some Underwear In The Mail.
The Canton Visit.
McGuire's Big Hit.
Sarah Ann.
Lost E-Mail and Death Threats.
Everybody Plays Volleyball.
Jimmy's Orange Welding Mask.
Blair Witch.
Schuman's U-Haul Blanket.
The Real World According To Buege.
Cocaine Steak.
Lost Digits.
Rain, Lightning, And A Concrete Pour.
Crawfish Boil.
Sticks In The Seat.
Noggin.
Forrest Broke Brian's Leg!
Get Your Hand Off Forrest's Thoat.
Canoeing With Jeff.
Thomas Saves The Pig.
Please Fix Your Burgers At The Creation Station.
Snow At Scarlett's.
Breakfast At Sav-More.

My wife is putting up her knitting needles. The sweater that she is working on for our son is very large, and she only has the back done. "I just need to take something in there," she tells me. She goes to a lady named Memory in Vestavia Hills who owns a yarn shop. She 'teaches' knitting, but I gather that it is more of what I would call a sewing circle. Ladies sit around and talk about their kids and grand kids, and this lady, Memory, helps them along with their projects.

"You bind off the first stitch," my wife explains as she sits, needle and yarn in hand, staring at a bent up cover of a pattern book enigmatically titled I Can't Believe I'm Knitting.

I'm staring at a relatively empty monitor, just these first words and a lot of icons. I've had a hard time writing this thing that I'm trying to write about you. I'm realizing that it was a long time ago. A lot has happened between then and now, and it is hard sometimes to put it all together in a sensible form. A lot of it is just not very consistent. Memories are about all that really connect me back, and the memories are stretching out and thinning every day.

My memories of you are disjointed. Some of them exhibit all of the qualities that people expect out you: the gentleman professor, the noble visionary, the unlikely genius. But other memories have nothing to do with those qualities, if they involve you at all. They are memories of an ordinary guy, of a friend, but not of the demigod into which you are evolving. They are also memories of an experience that have nothing to do with the noble mission of the Rural Studio. They are memories of growing up as much as they are of learning lessons. So I've been asking myself whether the things we remember of a person or an experience necessarily have to exhibit qualities of that experience, or are they merely suspended in it. Memories are ungrounded and with time they become anecdotal. They loose the significance that context gives them and become something different, more like sound-bites than complete thoughts.

My wife has put aside the sweater and picked up a circular needle with about 2 inches of unbleached cotton fabric hanging off of it. It is blanket, also for our unborn son. It is her filler project, and it is taking her longer than she would like because of its size.

"No more blankets," she says, smiling.

Her father died when she was a junior in high school. I've been talking to her about the things that I'm writing here. She tells me that she remembers him as much through other people's stories as she does through her own memories.

One person's story is their story -because they get a good response from it," she notes, "not necessarily because it is the truth."

Should I even try to interpret memories, or is it better to leave them alone? Raw memories arranged and rearranged are still just raw memories. The ways you situate ideas near each other only create the tensions and synergies of an interpretation, but they don't necessarily add truth or even clarify it. What can I possibly add to the value of a remembered experience--to the value of the memory after the fact--that doesn't somehow distort it?

It is easy to believe that we know someone better once they are dead. I was never sure I understood you entirely, and I felt like I knew you as well any of your students. I couldn't ever predict your reactions to things. Maybe my expectations were misaligned, but even now I'm not sure how. I wanted to impress you, I know that. Once you died I went through a phase in which all of the uncertainties surrounding your character, all of that mysterious stuff that made you unique, started to crystallize into a big vision of what you were trying to do, what you were trying to tell us. But it's easy to speak for and about someone who isn't around to defend himself from righteous proclamations and propositions and dissections and interpretations. I can say that you were larger than yourself, authentically unique, and no one will ever be able to sum up what you were about without somehow including your intangibility or unpredictability.

Still, so much is left unclear. There is a lot of dialogue about the strength of your character and vision. It must suck being dead. You can't defend yourself. People can speak wrongly on your behalf. They can profess to be your ambassadors to the living-interpreters for the afterlife, damnation by the living. You just can't move on, because everyone is going to dwell on the snapshot of you on your deathbed, unable to move beyond on

their own, wheels spinning carving out the ruts that mark your place in history, bolting you down, casting you into the present as the present moves rapidly forward and your legacy is stuck in the mouths of pundits. I can't nail down your spirit: it is ghostlike, uncertain, and, always slightly devious, it slips out of view just as I recognize it. I never really understood you, and it's that ambiguity that keeps me interested.

Anyone looking at your body of work needs to understand that it is more than just a snapshot of your career at its peak; they need to understand and believe that your teachings live on in the studio's continuing evolution and in students, past and present, who have gone onto careers both within and outside of the profession. It's not about architecture. The buildings were incidental. Our eyes have been opened to fresh ideas and to compassion, concepts that at times people seem to have written off as impractical or idealistic. Practice, empathy and vision can work together. Its not about a bottom line, the human spirit doesn't stop at the bottom line and it certainly isn't tied to it. We must stay fresh, explore new ideas, not get scared: fear feeds hate, fans negativity, and nurtures apathy.

We are all your products. Our collective life's works, if we direct our energy to the right places, have the ability to reach further than you could have imagined. But we've got to make the effort, whenever we can, because nobody else is going to get it done right, and they stand a good chance of messing it up. The key is getting started. Figure the thing out as you go and you'll do well as long as you are guided by a clear set of principals, and don't ever go backwards. These things you taught me.

My wife has knitted the entire sweater. It is in pieces: two sleeves, two front panels, and a back, and it is very large. Our son isn't due until September, and, historically, we have very small babies. She has to take the separate pieces to Memory to assemble it since she has yet to learn to crochet.

My wife knits and needs to learn to crochet--I would love to talk to you about how growing up is working out, I'm sure you'd find it funny. I'd like for you to have met my daughter, but I was only able to take her to your funeral. She's really damn cute.

31 May 03.

I'm sitting in Lucy's basement. Her son A.J. is lying on the couch watching a movie. It's pouring down rain. She asks if my truck windows are rolled up. I say no, but I'm too comfortable to do anything about it.

I know Lucy Harris, client and recipient of the Rural Studio's "Lucy House" (the Carpet House), because I was one of seven "Outreach" students who helped build the house last year. It's been almost two years since we first visited Mason's Bend where Sambo introduced us to Lucy, her husband, Anderson, and their four kids.

Lucy talks candidly today allowing me a precious insight into Sambo's own life and his innate ability to choose clients, students, and environments. Through Lucy and through Mason's Bend, we come to know the Rural Studio. And understand our responsibility as architects, as designers, as citizens.

The following is her own words, though it can't truly capture her laughter, expressions, and emotion:

I thank God for Mason's Bend. Everybody thought that it was a far-away place, which it is, you know. We call Greensboro "the city". But here, here it's wooded, and the dirt road, (it used to be one lane) well, it would get so muddy with red clay that when it rained you'd be prayin' and hopin' you wouldn't meet another car; or else you'd have to back up the whole way... It's the only place we've ever lived at, was Mason's Bend. It's our home, it's where our family's land that they bought is. One time we had thought maybe we move out of Mason's Bend...

The first time I got a chance to meet Mr. Sambo was down my parent's house. He had come down there and talked to them about buildin' them a house. My daddy was in the middle of building himself a house, which probably would never had got done because of finances and he was buildin' it with old stuff, no strong boards, you know... when Mr. Sambo said he was gonna build them a house and they's wouldn't have to pay nothing for it... well, it was just like a miracle because someone you never heard of just appears and then they go in and bless you with a house from the ground up. And from that day on that's how we got acquainted...Well, Mr. Sambo, he just fitted right in. He didn't make you feel discomfort in no kinda way. Because where we sat, he sat, where we ate, he ate. Even the "country" food. Yep, he tried everything and then acted like he enjoyed it whether he did or not — but he never made you feel less.

He built my mama's house, and then my father-in law's house, and one day he had told me, he said, "Lucy, I'm gonna build you a house." And I said "Well, I receive it." And he said, "Huh?" and I said, "I receive what you say. When it comes to pass I will receive it in my spirit." I was just so thankful that he had built my mother a house, I was just so thankful that he did that for her...Things came up and my sister truly needed a place to stay, so they built her a beautiful place. And then a basketball court for the kids. And then Mr. Sambo, well, he asked me to be a kind of spokesperson for the community, to see what we needed,

wanted. You see, I was still workin' right along with him. So they built the glass chapel, the community center. Where we pray; the kids, they eat lunch there in the summer, you know. And Sambo kept saying "I'm gonna build you a house," and I kept sayin' "I receive it."...

It was in his heart, he didn't have to make up nothing, he was himself, because a person that's not himself, they can pretend for a while, and then the real you will come afloat. But Mr. Sambo was the same person. Always. He had that sweet spirit about himself.

He came down to the house one day and he had brought this sketch. And he had said, "This here is gonna be your house." My heart just pounded on the inside, rejoicing. Oh, God, thank you. He was showin' me what he was gonna do. I never told him how to build it or nothin', but all my life I always wanted a house with a basement. So he was showin' me, and he said, "this is gonna be your basement." I never, never told him that I wanted a basement. When he said that, oh my God, now I know my dream's coming true! I couldn't believe that. A house with a basement. I always wanted a place that I could just get away. Where I could come and pray and not interrupt anybody. And now I have it...we love it.

My husband, Anderson, we've been married for seventeen years. He said he had "eyes" for me ever since I was 15. He had told God that if God gave me to him, he'd do good about me for the rest of his life. So me and him have been together ever since. I thank God for my relationship with him... and he spoils me. He's my soul mate...I have met Sambo's wife and family. I know Mr. Sambo had to have a good wife backing him, an understanding wife. For him being gone and working with other people, he had to have someone encouraging him on the other end, that kept his heart inspired. And I think that behind every good man is a good woman, you know. But for her I just say, her husband's work wasn't in vain, it still lives on and, truly, we appreciate her for letting us have a part of him because he gave himself to us. They say everything got a time and a season. God raised him up on the faith of the earth, put it in his heart to bless other people, not just, you know, a selfish blessing, not just to be seen or to be heard like that, but I really believe everything he did for people he did from the sincerity of his heart.

You know, Mason's Bend, it's a quiet area, and most people is family folk, family people. You look out for them, for each other...it's been that way ever since I can remember. Aunts, uncles, cousins...if you was at one of their houses, you'd be just like your own house. Whatever they had, we had. Someone always had "eyes" up on you.

Now, people from all over the world come to see the area, to see the houses, where people never thought they'd be. Now it's a better place to live with houses we'd never dreamt we could live in. Because of Mr. Sambo and the Rural Studio, other people try to have their houses lookin' better and their yards too. The whole thing has worked out to be a blessing for Mason's Bend. Because if someone cares about your community, you should care about it too.

– Kerry Larkin

Sambo Mockbee: Teacher Extraordinary

By William Levinson

In addition to his work at Auburn, Sambo Mockbee also taught at Harvard and at Yale, at Berkeley and at the University of Virginia. He had little patience for the legion of black clad professors who all seemed to say the same, stale unimaginative things. Sambo had a "fury" against what he called an "education of abstraction." He felt students should not just see a professor for an hour in a classroom setting, they should know what he was like outside and in all kinds of situations. At the Rural Studio, he offered himself up to his students twenty four hours a day.

I met Sambo in December 2000. I told him I wanted to write something about him. He invited me to come on down to Newbern. "We'll get in my new pick up truck and drive around and shoot the shit and then I'll turn you loose." When I arrived, he told me not to waste my money staying at a hotel and invited me to bunk with him at Spenser the remodeled 19th century Victorian where he stayed when he was in residence. For the next week, I followed him around and watched what he did from the time he got up in the morning until he made the steep climb up the stairs to his Spartan bedroom on the second floor, dog tired, legs swollen from the medication he was taking for his leukemia.

What follows is what I observed on the second night of my stay in the "war room" of Spenser House, the hub in those days of most of the activity at the Rural Studio.

8:30 p.m. Sambo is on the on the telephone with his wife, Jackie catching up on the news at his home in Canton, Mississippi. A second year student enters carrying a scale model of a proj-ect she'd been working on. Sambo hangs up the phone and warmly greets her. She places the model on the trestle table in front of him and announces it's a battered woman's shelter which consists of three structures surrounding a courtyard. Sambo takes it in. Although his manner is always genial and unhurried, when it comes to architecture he is quick and decisive.

He is bothered by something in the design and begins to question the young woman. She now informs him there is an entire complex of structures which fit over what he is looking at and proceeds to put them in place. The design is instantly transformed.

"Now this is complex," says Sambo, lighting up, and begins to pepper her with questions about the interior of the second story. In response, she produces a schematic drawing.

"The minute I see this," says Sambo, pointing to an awkward series of jogs designating doors and walls, "I know you haven't thought this part out. You've got a really brilliant design here, something truly interesting, but it's the details of the interior space that are going to make it or break it."

He urges her to go home and work on it. She says she has plans to go to Chicago for the weekend, but "guesses" she'll be taking it with her.

"Well, these are the decisions you have to make."

Earlier in the evening I watched Sambo with a stocky, serious young man with dark hair. He was having a problem with his project and was showing Sambo his renderings. Sambo looked them over and picked up a pen and began sketching over the student's design and in the margins around it, thinking out loud as he drew. From the other end of the "war room," Steve Hoffman, a former student who now taught at the Rural Studio, teasingly asked if Sambo was "telling" the student what to do. Sambo protested he was only making a "suggestion," and insisted that the young man was free to do whatever he wanted. Whenever he himself got stuck on a design he told the student, he looked to see "how high" he could take it or "how low" or "how wide." With a few swift movements of his pen, Sambo dropped the floor level of the design creating a double height ceiling which completely transformed the space. It stuck me as a special moment. The master not just critiquing the student, but passing on a personal, hard won insight about his craft to a worthy acolyte.

It's nine-thirty when the young woman with the battered women's shelter departs and Sambo who's been on the go now for nearly fourteen hours starts thinking about dinner, and we hea down the "dog trot" foyer to the long kitchen at the rear of Spenser House which has its own double height ceiling supported by barkless tree trunks fixed in the floor on concrete plinths.

We're about to start eating when another young woman arrives with a model of a community center and park and places it on the kitchen table. Sambo puts aside any thought of food and without the slightest hint of impatience begins to examine it. One section is still incomplete, she informs him, but Sambo likes it as is and finds it really engaging.

"I'll tell you what I don't like," he adds, "and that's the front façade. It's too symmetrical. Like a stage set." He remarks on the outstanding quality of the young woman's sketches and asks how a second year student happens to come by such ability. She informs him her father is a builder and speculates that perhaps she's inherited his facility. Sambo warns her that it is precisely for that reason she must be careful not to get into bad habits. He points to an aspect of her sketches which he says look more suited to cartoon drawing then shows her how to create more shading in another section so that the dark and light areas will blend into one another and not appear in such stark stark contrast. "This also gives more of a sense of volume," he explains. "Dark comes forward. Light recedes."

When they are finished, Sambo cajoles her into playing the piano for us. She mildly protests then sits at the upright piano in the foyer and plays a nocturne by Chopin. When she is finished we applaud and she leaves.

Nearly a year after Sambo's death, I am interviewing Johnny Parker, a former inmate at the State Cattle Ranch who now works at the Rural Studio (a whole other story) and in his south Alabama accent relates the following anecdote about Sambo the teacher. "One Friday night Sambo was getting all his stuff together getting ready to go home and one of the second year students comes up and says she's having problems with her watercolors. Sambo listens to her problem and tells her to go get it and sits there on the front porch of Spenser House and helps her for two hours. She was crying and everything so he stayed two more hours just to help her. When they get finished with it, Sambo's happy, she's happy, and Sambo says, 'I can go home.' That's just the way he was. No matter how busy he was he always made time for his students."

AVL-VILLE I

This is AVL-Ville's main site.
Here you'll find the atelier where all the products and works of art are designed
and produced, the Hall of Delights, the AVL Academy and the area where you can
live and build without needing a building or residence permit and where there
are no zoning laws.

AVL-VILLE II

This part of AVL-Ville is the home of the pioneer set.
The pioneer set is the easily dismantled farm which, along with all its tools and
equipment, can be transported in a shipping container and unpacked anywhere in the
world so a new farm can be started. Cultivation is to be carried out according to
organic principles and the products are intended for private consumption. This summer,
a small workshop is being set up to convert railway carriages, and the AVL canteen
will be open for snacks, pleasant recreation and special events.

PRE: *text*   On January 8, 2002, in the kitchen of the Spencer house in Newbern Alabama, the Rural Studio: Andrew Freear, Jay Sanders, Dick Hudgens, Ann Langford, Brenda Wilkerson, Melissa Denney, Johnny Parker and Dufess (Johnny's dog), 14 thesis students, 8 outreach students, and myself, met for the first time since Sambo Mockbees' death a month earlier. Among many words of commiseration and remembrance I offered the following:

Sambo was a husband, a father, a teacher, and a citizen architect. He knew that buildings had the capacity to connect people to people, and people to places, so that they know where they are. Knowing where you are is important. It is easy to forget you are somewhere and not anywhere. Sambo knew that architecture was a way for non-pilots to elevate themselves so that they could see where they are, and hence know a little better who they are. They say that a good teacher will take you to another place... a great teacher will show you a new place, right where you stand.

While it was a somber morning in Hale County there was a quiet determination behind the tears that reflected work to be finished, *citizen architects* to be educated, and the need to *proceed boldly*. This need felt like gravity and oncoming weather; familiar and scary in the inertia of things set in motion. Joseph Campbell said praise the culture that honors heroes, and in the same breath said pity the culture that needs them.

The Last Ten Years and The Next...   The Rural Studio stands unique in architectural education. The premise remains a simple one: the education of *citizen* architects. The method is direct: build what you design and build community as well as buildings. Over the last ten years the Rural Studio has completed over 30 design/build projects involving over four hundred students. It has also facilitated many more *neck down* repair and small community projects, This work has happened through the agency of a handful of faculty, staff and clients. In addition hundreds of community members, city and county officials, visiting architects, scholars, and visitors from all over the world made contributions. A generation of *citizen architects* have been educated.

In the next ten years the Rural Studio will design/build: ten homes for low-income Hale county families, thirty community and institu-

tional projects, and will implement, organize, and contribute to a large number of *neck down* and community projects throughout the Blackbelt region of Alabama. The program will participate in the education of another four hundred architects. The Outreach Program will allow artists and students from around the world to contribute to the extended community through multi-disciplinary projects and research. A newly formed Rural Studio Advisory group will help the faculty, staff, and students proceed with forethought, imagination, and critical evaluation. This group includes Sambo's wife Jackie Mockbee, as well as local and national friends and alumni of the Rural Studio. Carol, Sambo and Jackie's daughter, and Julius, Sarah Ann and Margaret's sister, will be a student at the Rural Studio this year.

Proceeding Boldly: *working theories*   Architecture, for the most part, has long since lost its social pretense. Environmental determinism is dead. Are not human aspirations and actions constrained or even dictated by their economic, political, and cultural circumstances and not by the buildings they inhabit. Or, to quote Marx, "Men make their own history, but... they do not make it under circumstances chosen by themselves." [Watts] Nowadays it is presumptuous, even suspicious, to help someone. Therefore new architecture and social practice can never come from within these existing conditions. It must continually be created anew from afar. The *modern project* reflects this through an abstraction that results in a productive distance that allows for new possibilities to be seen. Architecture survives, but often disembodied. Besides: the practice of architecture has become an itinerate profession. Abstractions allow us to bring pictures home and computers allow us to inhabit representations as if they are places. Architects don't build buildings; they make drawings and [computer] models. Still: there are other ways that new possibilities can be captured.

Building   The late Los Angeles architect Rudolph Schindler said, "Theory is good. Building is better." Building, historically a significant activity, often exemplified technology and progress. Building has since become a commodity. The result is construction: a multi-billion dollar industry that institutionalizes "the belief that the means of a buildings production [are] without consequence to whatever meanings might be associated with the [architecture]." Yet building continues as a medieval activity that cannot be justified on economic terms because the profit is embedded in things that are difficult to quantify and relationships that are beyond the immediate scope of the project. I draw the distinction between building and construction from a discussion by a friend Dan Willis in his book the <u>Emerald City</u> about the difference between work and labor. Labor is socialized, unionized, and valued on efficiency. Work, on the other hand is risky, inefficient, and is almost always in some way a gift. It results in a product that "exceeds the value of the effort that went into making it," and stands as a visual and *working* manifestation of the effort and sacrifice of the collective desire to improve our condition. It becomes meaningful, and even beautiful because of this. The product also demonstrates this. Willis uses the example of shinned shoes that at one time were a demonstration of care. Now, when shoes can be made permanently shinny they may indicate, but they cannot demonstrate. Construction may indicate, but it cannot demonstrate that the process of *building* can be significant and add meaning and beauty to the result.

Art is lonely business. Building at the Rural Studio, on the other hand, is pursued as a collective activity. It includes the students (often their parents and siblings), the faculty, and the client(s). It also involves citizens of the immediate area, and an extended circle that includes visiting architects, engineers, and foundation/corporate, and individual donors. Companies from around the country routinely donate materials and building products. Rural Studio Director Andrew Freear directs this work with passion and commitment. The belief is that the work is significant and builds both buildings and community. It also develops in young students an ethic of design that is collaborative in nature and gives weight to an idea of sustainable practice. This idea recognizes that the human need to do significant work may be as important an environmental resource, as the rain forest. [Willis] All of this may be a romantic lament for things lost in the face of accelerating change and globalization. The audaciousness of results, according to students and clients of the Rural Studio, suggest otherwise.

Social Work, "you are innocent when you dream" Critics of the Rural Studio point out the complexity of the social issues surrounding mostly middle class white students and faculty doing work for a predominately African American community that is potent with the realities of Southern history, racism, and poverty. Admittedly these issues are complex and are susceptible to practices that historically have excluded minority groups replicating the very social inequities they mean to alleviate. Two things are important in regard to this serious question. First: the primary mission of the Rural Studio is the education of *citizen architects*. The added social benefit to the student and the community is not in addition to this mission, but the result of architecture practiced in this way. When architecture is practiced from a position of advocacy the material, formal, and expressive potentials expand. Second: the Rural Studio has spent 10 years becoming a part of the community it works in. To be a part of a community is to belong to it: "this contravenes instant joining and easy leave taking." Sambo was more direct: "Architecture won't begin to alleviate all of these social woes. But what is necessary is a willingness to seek solutions to poverty in its own context, not outside it… with knowledge based on human contact and personal realization applied to the work and place."

Education It would only be slightly unfair to describe most current architectural education as educating students about people, buildings, and the environment without the people, the building, and the influence of the environment. Architectural education, the practice, and the profession are recursive. As always, education is to blame and our only hope.

Current models of ecology suggest that diversity = survival and complexity = life. An ecology of design education might be diversity = creativity. The Rural Studio will continue its contribution to the broader vision of the School of Architecture at Auburn University. Along with the Center for Architecture and Urban Studies (the Urban Studio) in Birmingham and through the four professional programs, the School provides a model for a new contemporary environmental design practice – one that is interdisciplinary, diverse, and complex. This *emergent collective practice* is based on the fact that we can do things together that we can't do alone. It is not a coincidence that the Rural Studio comes from this school and that it recalls the childhood dreams of climbing great mountains, building tall towers, and changing the world.

– Bruce Lindsey, Head, School of Architecture,
  Co-Director Rural Studio, Auburn University

Original photo by Vincent J. Varga

HOW I WISH I'D MET SAMBO MOCKBEE, SEEN HIM IN ACTION, HEARD HIM INTERACT, WATCHED HIM GO ABOUT HIS SELF-APPOINTED MISSION. As it is, my one-day visit to the Rural Studio - less than a year ago, after his death-comes back in snapshot form. A bit out of focus, as we careened through the landscape's country roads to see just one more project before dark... The snapshots weren't the photographs I took, since I ran out of film, and they were pretty unsatisfactory, but images in the mind, the memory. They blur with childhood memories, visiting my grandparents at Tougaloo College in Jackson, Mississippi, being the only white child at my fourth birthday party, a summer on the Bayou Lafitte with my best friend's family, driving for a few years from New Orleans to Maine through the rural south, still an exotic terrain for my New England family - long-ago images brought home more recently by Beverly Buchanan's photographs and sculptures. My view of poverty, before political awakening, was mixed with romantic longings for a "country life."

Aside from coming away from Hale County with the most enormous admiration for what the Rural Studio has done and is doing, one big question keeps surfacing: Why the hell isn't this being done everywhere? Each region deserves its own version. I dream of a New Mexico Rural Studio (my home state has a terrible problem with affordable housing) and one for Maine and one for upstate New York and so forth and so on. I imagine the wonderful breadth such a model would provide for the future of architecture. It set me thinking.

I talked with a student in Newbern about trailers, recalling J.B. Jackson's stubborn fondness for the much maligned manufactured housing. In New Mexico (where he lived) the white and gray - not to mention the purple and bright green-trailers stand out like sore thumbs in the low-slung brown landscape. Recently attempts have been made to accommodate or upscale with the addition of plastic vigas and adobe colored metal. A step in the right direction, but why not re-invent the mobile home and the trailer park landscape?

The Rural Studio puts put into practice everything I've been preaching about for most of my writing life: Respect for community, the artist's social responsibility, esthetic integrity, concern for and knowledge of the way people form places, art as process, the down-to-earth joys of an esthetic inseparable from ethics. Mockbee spoke movingly about "architecture without pretense" and called for "subversive leadership," for architects who "can step over the threshold of injustice" and avoid being stunned by the power of technology and affluence, architects with a "willingness to seek solutions to poverty in its own context." (I wish I'd been able to ask him the tough questions about class, about the ups and downs of relationships between the Rural Studio and its clients, about how tradition and habit reclaims modernist ideals – especially as more and more visitors trouped through people's houses.) The poetry with which he spoke about his work translated into the prose of raw, recycled, innovative materials without losing its power.

For years I've wondered why most art schools have resisted so vehemently the models provided by such exemplary community modernists as Suzanne Lacy, John Malpede, Rick Lowe and many others. The option, even the opportunity to work in the real world, to build something meaningful with others, is still lacking for most would-be artists and architects. And yet such opportunities make such a difference. They change, and charge, the creative mind whether or not the vision is consistently pursued. (I know. The American Friend Service Committee provided me with such an experience the year I graduated from college; work in a Mexican village changed my life the way radical politics and feminism did a decade later.) Somehow we have to break the strangle hold of self-serving, self-centered, and self-censoring arts education.

Surely Mockbee's ideas are bigger than he was. For all his famous warmth and ingenuity, the Rural Studio continues without him. Why can't its principles spread too? With pessimism of the intellect (apologies to Gramsci), I wonder if this country still has the moral fiber to think in terms of "decency" and honesty." With optimism of the will, I believe it does.

– *Lucy R. Lippard*

Para dois (For two), 2003, Acrylic on Canvas, 118 x 75 inches

A Watermelon Lunch

I was visiting Birmingham at the occasion of the opening of my exhibition at the Birmingham Museum of Art in July, 2001. David Moos asked me to drive with him to visit with the architect Samuel Mockbee. The idea was to introduce me to his architecture / social project and to have lunch with him. I never suspected that this day would become very special... a moment in your life that you never forget. We met him at his office, where he conducts all of his projects: Renovating old, abandonned historical houses; constructing new homes, specially designed and developed by his students at the university, from recycled materials, which provide dignified spaces for impoversihed families... his projects were impressive. But, I really knew that I was infront of a man who was a true "character" when we had our "water-mellow" lunch! We were sitting at a big, warm table with a wonderful view and ready for our lunch when a strong black man arrived with two beautiful watermelons and abruptly cut them into irregular pieces and offered them to us as a meal. This image is vivid in my mind as a Gauguin painting. The red with green. The wood. The sun. The black man.

Thanks Samuel.

– Beatriz Milhazes

ARCHITECTURAL
RECORD

HOUSES

04 | 1997

$7.00

A PUBLICATION OF THE MCGRAW-HILL COMPANIES

Suzannah Lessard
on the Symbolism of Houses

Special Section: **Record Lighting**

From Pickwick Lake, the prominent tin roof seems to float above the substantial brick base, supported only by coke bottle green glass walls. The house has become a local landmark, visible for miles on the lake. Locals call it the "arrow house" since it looks like an arrow pointing directly toward Florence Alabama from the air.

The house was famous even before construction began with the publication of the original plan in GA Houses 45 Project 1995. The original carport design (later changed) is very similar to the Harris (Butterfly) House. Rising 150 feet from the surface of the lake, with a view extending for miles into Tennessee, Mississippi, and Alabama, the house is in many ways a grand version of the Yancey Chapel. This house represents the culmination of a twelve-year collaboration between Sam Mockbee and his partner Coleman Coker. Sam was quoted as saying that Coleman was the most talented man he ever met.

I met Sam Mockbee for the first time at a party in Memphis. He was very eager to do this project and stated that he and Coleman would give us a world famous house if we hired them. Although he later denied making such a grandiose statement, he was true to his word.

My brother and I purchased the lot at Shiloh Falls several years before. We were impressed with the sheer beauty of the site and had no immediate plans to develop it. Later we planed to build a serviceable vacation house. A friend of ours suggested that we not waste such a spectacular site on a mundane house, but consider hiring an important architect to design a significant building.

We researched the subject and even traveled to the most famous modern American house, Wright's Falling Water. After a visit with Sam in Canton MS and a tour of the Barton House, we decided to hire him rather than a better-known architect. Sam's eloquent explanation of space, volume, and views convinced us that Sam and Coleman were at a pivotal point in their careers. As such, our house would be more significant than just one in a series. Since we were not actually going to live in the house, we could take the risk of allowing them a free hand in the design. We have never regretted our decision.

– *Rushton (and James) Patterson*

Throughout history God has chosen individuals to speak to the human race revealing something

Mississippi River
Huck and Jim
Black Warrior Turtle Diadem

To know by name
is a different game,
gathering everyone
under the mast.
Bobby,
Randy,
Sandy
B.B., Bob, Greg
Coleman, Bill, DK and Frank
not so fast
not so fast
and hundreds of
thousands of
millions of others
who'll come in just after the show
and oh yeah
then there's Walker
and James
and there's Bill
and there's Tim
and those photos we all know.

Mississippi River
Huck and Jim
Black Warrior Turtle Diadem

After all of the eating and working and playing
and laughing and dreaming and sleeping;
Calling us; calling us; the Samuels are calling us;
Space and Race and a Noble Place.
Wacked on the Edge
neither Safe nor Sane,
America's Greatest
Sambo and Twain.
Both said it was easy
to do what they did,
listen, be honest, learn how to live.
Heed the Hierophants' message:
Its OK
Its OK
IT is OK
to Give.

8/11/02

by Richard I. Pigford, AIA

about His nature, and His intention for our relationship with Him and with each other.

"II Samuel"

Mississippi River
Huck and Jim
Black Warrior Turtle Diadem

Lead by a man,
in the palm of his hand
to a threshold we each know and fear.
that place on our mind
we're all seeking to find;
our nature's listening ear.

Mississippi River
Huck and Jim
Black Warrior Turtle Diadem

In Paris or Rome
or Warsaw or Cypress
or Corinth or Memphis
or home,
the language
old
worn out
and cold
the everyday we all know,
is raised up by a genius
in a story we're told
that touches and awakens our soul.

Yeah, its one for the money
and two for the show
and we're skipping along
with no place to go,
just following the road
all the way to the end
down by the rivers bend.
To a place
we are led
out from under the shed
cleaver students knowing
the we and the them;
the we and the them;
the we and the them;
the day long
then somewhere on the path
we turn the corner and gasp
to discover the we
has a name...well its...
Huck and its
me
and the them...
well you see..
they're
Alberta
and Lucy
and Ora Lee.

Week after week
you kiss your youth
and go marching off to war,
where the battle line
is in your mind,
and there's no place
to hide from the truth.
The journey
the battleground
the charge up the hill
a raft and a river
the human will;
in hay bales and earth
in beaver sticks
gourds
and worn out tires
lie our noble spirit,
our common birth.

Adrift near the
Shoals of Indifference

by Charles Reeve

As adages go, "once a Marxist, always a Marxist" lacks the homeliness and currency of cozily familiar sayings like "a stitch in time saves nine" or "a change is as good as a rest," but it explains better than any of its well-worn counterparts why I am attracted by the edges of photographs of Rural Studio projects.

The many pictures of the justly celebrated Mason's Bend Community Center, which Rural Studio completed in 2000, are excellent examples. Famously, this meeting pavilion/chapel triumphantly combines aesthetics with make-do in a stunning glass wall fabricated from eighty Chevrolet Caprice windshields that Jon Schumann, a thesis student involved in the design, got from a junkyard for one hundred and twenty dollars.[1] Pull back from the building, though, look off to the sides or into the background, and you'll see that the proud structure sits on an unkempt lot — a mud patch, really — surrounded by a dirt road.

Or look at the images of the house, also in Mason's Bend, that Mockbee and his students built for Sheperd and Alberta Bryant and their grandchildren in 1993 – 1994. Mockbee had just founded the Rural Architecture Studio as a partial answer to his question "How do we, as architects, step over the threshold of injustice and address the true needs of a neglected family, particularly the needs of their children?"[2] The Bryant House was the first Rural Studio project and, like the community center, brilliantly marries design with an almost impossible economic efficiency. Fabricated from stucco-covered hay bales, the dwelling features a spacious, sheltered front porch to accommodate family activities. Set off by a jaunty smokehouse designed and built by Rural Studio student Scott Stafford, the setting seems pleasant, joyful, even amazing.

Until, that is, the Marxism I acquired in my early years of graduate school draws my attention away from the smokehouse to the other side of the lot, where the Bryants' previous dwelling stands. No polite adjectives capture this structure's desperation. It has none of the humor implied by "ramshackle" or "rickety," none of the romance or picturesque-ness suggested — however obliquely — by "run-down" or "dilapidated." It's completely fucked-up, barely a building. That the Bryants lived here with their grandchildren defies belief. "Children should be the common denominator in every decision we make as a society," Mockbee once observed regarding the Bryants' former living situation. "The eleven million children living below the poverty line are an indictment of our material affluence and lack of caring."[3]

In other words, the Bryants are far from alone in their destitution, especially in Hale County where Mason's Bend is located and where the poverty rate — almost twenty-seven percent — is more than twice the national average.[4] The region's need for adequate housing, let alone for homes that give their occupants a sense of uniqueness and pride, far surpasses the Rural Studio's capacity. Even in tiny Mason's Bend (population about one hundred), two families needed their assistance. That probably means four or five families require their help among the two hundred and fifty residents of Newbern, home of the Rural Studio's offices, and another ten or twelve families down the road at Akron (population around six hundred), where Mockbee's students converted a ruined storefront into a Boys and Girls Club. Even at double its current output, the Rural Studio would need nearly a decade to meet the housing needs of these towns. And then there's the rest of the county…

Despite these challenging circumstances, Hale is far from the poorest county in the United States: the poverty rates in Zavala County, Texas and East Carrall Parish, Louisiana are just under and just over forty percent, respectively; in Starr County, Texas, arguably the nation's poorest, the poverty rate reaches an appalling forty-five percent.[5] The Rural Studio isn't on its own in trying to house the nation's worst-off citizens, but clearly demand for this assistance far outstrips supply. And that's what I see intruding into the photographs of Mockbee's work: the cars up on cinder blocks and the fallen-down shacks that remind us how many people still tremble on poverty's stormy ocean. In this context, the Rural Studio's glowing jewels are like lighthouses, guiding us passed the shoals of indifference and pointing the way to a future of hope.

[1] Andrea Oppenheimer Dean and Timothy Hursley, *Rural Studio: Samuel Mockbee and an Architecture of Decency* (Princeton Architectural Press, 2002): 49-50.
[2] Lori Ryker and Randolph Bates, "Interview with Samuel Mockbee," in *Mockbee Coker: Thought and Process*, Lori Ryker, ed., (Princeton Architectural Press, 1995): 95.
[3] ibid.
[4] U.S. Census Bureau, "Population by Poverty Status in 1999 for Counties," *Census 2000 Sample Demographic Profiles* (U.S. Census Bureau, 2000): Table DP-3.
[5] U.S. Census Bureau, *Small Area Income and Poverty Estimates: Counties That Could Be Identified As The Poorest County in the U.S. in 1999* <www.census.gov/hhes/www/saipe/poorcty.html>.

Method and Madness

Most people think they have to choose between reality and fantasy. In a sense, the whole purpose of childhood is the slow and often painful separation of children from their dreams. And if that doesn't work, there's always psychoanalysis later on. We strive for rationality, for a sense of order and purpose. We want to be able to discuss our goals in the clear light of day.

Our society makes some room for people who don't want to leave their dreams behind, safely stored in sleep. They can be artists, writers, or musicians but not much else. Certainly nothing practical. We don't want people who have trouble distinguishing images from things driving our buses, trimming our trees, or installing our phones. Plato came down hard on these types and we still do.

So imagine an architect, not just an architect but a community builder and an advocate for social change, whose work depended on an engine of fantasy known almost only to himself. Who saw in his colleagues and clients embodiments of fantastical characters imbued with mythic purpose. Whose work in the world, celebrated as a model for progressive design, building and education, may have been simply the cast off foam from a vast imaginative sea.

This was Samuel Mockbee. When I went to see Sambo in the summer of 2001, we spent a day driving around Newbern and adjacent towns, visiting the inhabitants of half-a-dozen of the great Rural Studio-designed homes. The picture I formed of his project was one of almost utopian clarity. Here was a man with the vision, the will, and the resources to change a corner of the world. And to do so with as simple an idea as dignity. It all seemed so open and clear, yet there was madness to his method

At the end of our long, hot day together, Sambo decided to take me to his studio, which was not, as I had expected, a space devoted to architectural models and sketches. No, it was a place of fantasy: raw, mythic, uncensored images of the people we had just seen, the everyday inhabitants of the Rural Studio homes. Painted, collaged, and cobbled together from branches and other found materials, these portraits and tableaux presented Sambo's inner vision of his clients revealed as characters in an uncertain yet timeless drama of passion, love, and pain.

I never knew Sambo well, but on that sultry summer afternoon, I felt certain that the world described in these pictures was as real, if not more so, to him than the world of projects, grants, and classes that had won him so many important, and well-deserved accolades. Sambo was a secret shaman. Alone, he conjured spirits, coaxing them towards the light. In the company of others, he demonstrated how to build a better home.
– *Larry Rinder*

A Tribute To **SAMBO MOCKBEE**
by William A. Ryan

Aristotle wrote," Whatever we learn to do, we learn by actually doing it; men come to be builders by building, and harp players by playing the harp. In the same way, by doing just acts, we come to be just; ...and by doing brave acts, we become brave." These words describe the philosophy of Samuel (Sambo) Mockbee. Sambo brought the Rural Studio and its students to Hale County to learn by doing. Restoring "Old South" buildings in Greensboro was the focus of the first class of Rural Studio students who were to experience hands-on learning. Many such buildings needed this restoration, but Sambo soon learned of more pressing needs that the Rural Studio could address. These were the needs of Hale County's "invisible people." Utilizing the learn-by-doing model, his students learned to create more livable spaces for people. In partnership with the Hale County Department of Human Resources, the Rural Studio provided much needed improvements to a woman's home. These improvements allowed her to retain custody of her children who were in danger of being removed because she had inadequate housing. The students also remodeled a room in the house of a 90-year-old man who was about to freeze. They created a warm, dry space so that he could continue to live in the house where he was born. The Rural Studio met the needs of these citizens, and at the same time provided students with an opportunity to learn about creating livable and nurturing spaces. Sambo learned of the squalid conditions in which an elderly couple were living and trying to care for three of their grandchildren. Sambo believed that all children should have a warm, safe place to

g my contribution for the Mockbee exhibit.

to the Hale County community. I trust that

nk you also for choosing Sambo's work in

e news about the county is so rare. If I may

contest me. In the meantime, I am

live. Sambo's philosophy and this family's needs brought about construction of the now famous hay house. This began the tradition of building "charity houses." Four have been built in Mason's Bend (Sambo's adopted neighborhood) and two in other communities.

The Rural Studio also created public spaces such as the award winning tire chapel, the Akron pavilion, the HERO Family Resource Center (which began the partnership between HERO and the Rural Studio), the chapel at Mason's Bend, and the Akron Boys and Girls Club Building and Akron Senior Citizen's Center. These are all examples of projects completed by the Rural Studio to assist the citizens of Hale County. Few, if any, of these would have been undertaken had Hale County not been blessed with the presence of Sambo and the Rural Studio. In designing and building these buildings, Sambo's students learned not only how to design livable spaces but how to be brave citizens of a community. The partnership between the Rural Studio, HERO and the citizens of Hale County is making possible the sustainable revitalization of Hale County. The Knowledge Café—Community Career Resource Center of the HERO campus will provide the classroom for workforce development classes to further empower people. Sambo the architect had a vision of the Rural Studio program. He designed and modified the program, always working to ensure its existence and growth. His skill as an artist allowed him to paint a picture for prospective donors convincing them to support the continuing work of the Rural

Studio. I know he was equally happy and at ease with everyone he met—from the people of Mason's Bend to Oprah.

He inculcated his students with his vision for any building—it has to be warm, dry, and noble. They in turn learned that designing simple projects for truly appreciative people could be very rewarding. Equally important to the Hale County community was Sambo's vision of the County as it should be. Sharing similar visions of the "new" Hale County is what brought Sambo and me together. We talked many times about particular projects but the feeling of brotherhood I had with him was based on our shared vision of what Hale County could and should be and how we could make our visions a reality. I know that he loved his family and Auburn University. He also loved the Rural Studio and he struggled to maintain and expand the program.

Thomas Paine wrote," I love a man that can smile in trouble, that can gather strength from distress, and grow brave by reflection. 'Tis the business of little minds to shrink, but he whose heart is firm, and whose conscience approves his conduct, will pursue his principles unto death." We all remember with fondness the times we shared with Sambo, enjoying his humor, discussing politics, or what the next need the students would attack, or addressing challenges that arose in ongoing projects. He had no doubt that he was right in his ideals, opinions, or actions and, as we know, he worked toward attaining his goals until the end.

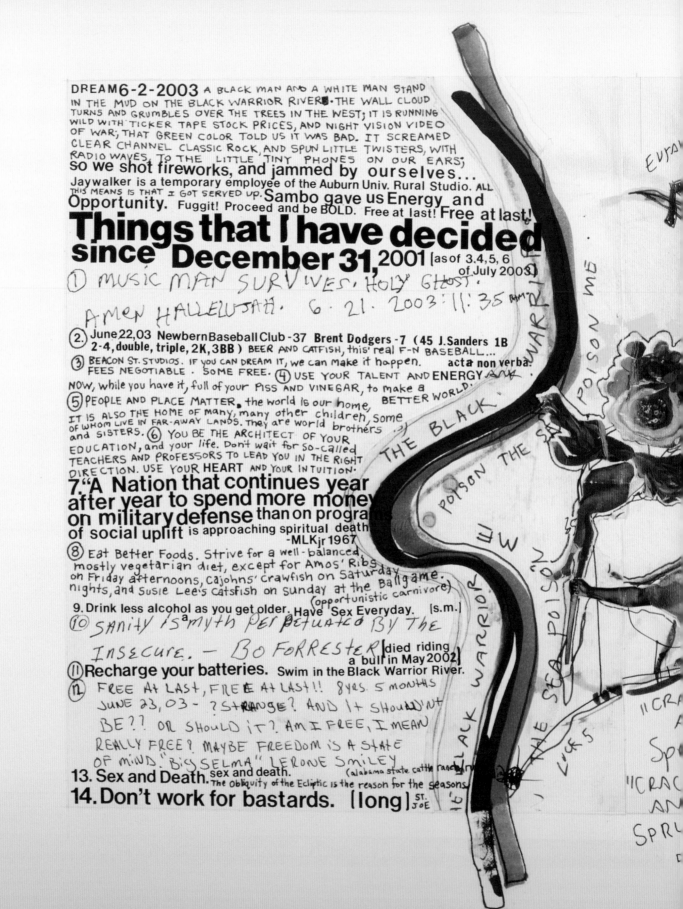

DREAM 6-2-2003 A BLACK MAN AND A WHITE MAN STAND IN THE MUD ON THE BLACK WARRIOR RIVER. THE WALL CLOUD TURNS AND GRUMBLES OVER THE TREES IN THE WEST; IT IS RUNNING WILD WITH TICKER TAPE STOCK PRICES, AND NIGHT VISION VIDEO OF WAR; THAT GREEN COLOR TOLD US IT WAS BAD. IT SCREAMED CLEAR CHANNEL CLASSIC ROCK, AND SPUN LITTLE TWISTERS, WITH RADIO WAVES, TO THE LITTLE TINY PHONES ON OUR EARS; so we shot fireworks, and jammed by ourselves...

Jaywalker is a temporary employee of the Auburn Univ. Rural Studio. ALL THIS MEANS IS THAT I GOT SERVED UP. Sambo gave us Energy and Opportunity. Fuggit! Proceed and be BOLD. Free at last! Free at last!

Things that I have decided
since December 31, 2001 [as of 3,4,5,6 of July 2003]

① MUSIC MAN SURVIVES, HOLY GHOST.

AMEN HALLELUJAH. 6·21·2003: 11:35 am?

② June 22,03 Newbern Baseball Club -37 Brent Dodgers -7 (45 J. Sanders 1B 2-4, double, triple, 2K, 3BB) BEER AND CATFISH, this' real F-N BASEBALL...

③ BEACON ST. STUDIOS. IF YOU CAN DREAM IT, we can make it happen. acta non verba. FEES NEGOTIABLE. SOME FREE. ④ USE YOUR TALENT AND ENERGY NOW, while you have it, full of your PISS AND VINEGAR, to make a BETTER WORLD.

⑤ PEOPLE AND PLACE MATTER, the world is our home, IT IS ALSO THE HOME OF many, many other children, some OF WHOM LIVE IN FAR-AWAY LANDS. They are world brothers and SISTERS. ⑥ YOU BE THE ARCHITECT OF YOUR EDUCATION, and your life. Don't wait for so-called TEACHERS AND PROFESSORS TO LEAD YOU IN THE RIGHT DIRECTION. USE YOUR HEART AND YOUR INTUITION.

7. "A Nation that continues year after year to spend more money on military defense than on programs of social uplift is approaching spiritual death"
-MLK jr 1967

⑧ Eat Better Foods. Strive for a well-balanced, mostly vegetarian diet, except for Amos' Ribs on Friday afternoons, Cajohns' crawfish on Saturday nights, and Susie Lee's Catfish on Sunday at the Ballgame. (opportunistic carnivore)

9. Drink less alcohol as you get older. Have Sex Everyday. [s.m.]

⑩ SANITY IS a myth PERPETUATED BY THE INSECURE. — BO FORRESTER [died riding a bull in May 2002]

⑪ Recharge your batteries. Swim in the Black Warrior River.

⑫ FREE AT LAST, FREE AT LAST!! 8 yrs. 5 months JUNE 23,03 - ? STRANGE? AND It SHOULDN'T BE?! OR SHOULD iT?. AM I FREE, I MEAN REALLY FREE? MAYBE FREEDOM IS A STATE OF MIND. "Big SELMA" LERONE SMILEY (alabama state cattle ranch)

13. Sex and Death. sex and death. The Obliquity of the Ecliptic is the reason for the seasons.

14. Don't work for bastards. [long] ST. JOE

It was the dog days of the early nineties. In the UK, the death throes of true Thatcherism were being announced as an ineffectual Conservative Government attempted to wrap her iron fist in a softer glove. But the damage was done. A lasting damage. The world had bought the lie, promulgated by Thatcher and Reagan, that because the free market was based on rational – for which read 'neutral' – principles of exchange it stood outside the political realm. Buildings, as part of that exchange system, are thus reduced to objects of capital, and at a stroke supposedly divested of any social role. It was in the eighties that architects finally relinquished their political responsibility and capitulated to the insatiable demands of the marketplace. A few glamourous arts projects provided aesthetic distraction, a few technologically advanced buildings suggested progress was being made – but nothing could really disguise the malaise.

It was in those dog days that we went to a lecture in Chicago by a big Southern man with a big beard. Samuel Mockbee. Never heard of him before. But that lecture was one of those moments of revelation when what one has clumsily been thinking about is both articulated intellectually and enacted practically. In the lecture Mockbee contrasted his work – "for the poorest man in the world" – with that of Michael Hopkins who was then building for "the richest woman in the world" (the Queen). He contrasted his vision of a social and political role for architecture with Hopkins' denial of such a role. Afterwards we wrote to Sambo and asked if we could publish his lecture; in our subsequent exchanges, and engagement with his work, Sambo became a mentor. Funny to have a mentor that one has never met, but such is the power of his work that we feel we know him well.

How, it may be asked, could work that is so marginal be so powerful? The Rural Studio works on the margins in every way. Spatially, they removed themselves from the centre of institutional control, taking students away from the comfort of pedagogic structure and authority. Materially, the Studio turns away from the limits of the centre (lets face it, there is only so much one can do with brick, steel, glass, wood and concrete) and scavenges the edges for inspiration. Socially, the Studio engages with communities consigned by poverty to that

It is now twenty years since the publication of Frampton's seminal essay on Critical Regionalism. The trouble then as now was that, despite Frampton's Frankfurt School influences, his regionalism was not actually that 'critical', relying more on aesthetics and tectonics than a political engagement with place. The work of the Rural Studio fulfils the promise of the term. The Studio produces buildings tied to their place, to their time and to their people - buildings which then empower their users. It is likely that the work of the Rural Studio will be held up as an exemplar of how to respond to a world of diminishing resources and increasing poverty gaps. In its dialogue with the local, the architecture - as product and process - will also be seen as a pioneering counterpoint to the homogenising tendencies of globalisation, a critical regionalism in the true sense of the word critical. It is here that Mockbee's contribution shows both depth and breadth. Breadth because in its engagement with wider forces it provides an example as to how others may operate beyond the specifics of Hale County. Depth because work of such complexity, and in its attention to the making, does not arise out superficial encounters with context; it comes from a profound understanding of the issues at stake in the processes of architecture.

Hopkins is far from the only architect from among the great and good to be guilty of this - but his clever combination of a soothing, conservative, aesthetic with technological sophistication is exemplary of a certain kind of distraction from wider social issues.

Scavenging round the edges like Mockbee, our own work employs found materials - sandbags, railway sleepers, straw and quilted cloth. 9 Stock Orchard Street, 2001, Sarah Wigglesworth Architects.

STRONG MARGINS

JEREMY TILL &
SARAH WIGGLESWORTH

The causes of the malaise in the architectural profession may be traced back to education. Four weeks into first year and students are exposed to the barbarity of the review/crit/jury. Power, hormones, fear, vanity, genius and individuality form a rich mix that sets the ethos for what is to come. Architectural education is still guided by the Victorian values of the (male) individual genius architect silently supplying aesthetic delight for rich patrons. The Rural Studio explicitly challenges these paradigms. It champions collaboration, communication, and process over product. It exposes students to a range of issues that they are sheltered from in normative architectural education – group working, social responsibility, lateral thinking, building skills, new ways of building procurement, sustainability, contingent creativity But at the same time one should not get too misty-eyed and see it as a completely non-authoritarian structure. Mockbee and his successors are far from shrinking violets; one needs this overarching vision (and it is vision not mindless control) to avoid the work descending to a level of worthy mediocrity as so easily could have happened.

There is the temptation when describing the Rural Studio to use words such as 'worthy', 'decent', 'honest' - liberal sentiments that invite us to see the work as part of the centre. In fact the Studio is more radical; operating from its strong margins, it produces work that can hold its own in any architectural beauty contest (the final objects are spatially and technically innovative), but also providing lessons for the centre to open up its eyes to wider possibilities.

forgotten territory, that terrible analogy, of the other sides of the tracks. Constructionally, the Studio uses marginal labour, some unskilled (students), some of it disenfranchised (prisoners). Geographically, Hale County is off the national radar. Economically, the Studio operates beyond the limits of the market, offering a service to those who could otherwise not afford it and funding it through soft sources. Pedagogically, it challenges many of the accepted norms of educational behaviour. Margins all round.

Too often the work on the margins is marginalised, pushed off into a corner, treated with disdain or patronized with interest, where it is rarely effective in making changes. However, another reading of the margins, that of authors such as bell hooks, suggests that there is a latent strength in the margins. The first strength is that it is only from the margins that one can clearly view the centre, and thus unravel all its closures, corruptions and limits. The movement suggested by this unraveling is not that the margins should move inwards to be accommodated by the centre (because that leads to a homogenizing suppression), but rather that the centre should disperse to accept the multiple values and diverse cultures that the margins address. A second strength lies in the freedoms that the margins offer away from the normative concerns of the centre; the margins offer, for bell hooks, "a space of radical openness".

It is these two strengths – of reformulation and freedom – that Mockbee initiated within the Rural Studio. His legacy lies not just in the continuing, and continually inspirational, work of the Rural Studio, but in asking such major questions of the centre. In particular his call to recognise the social context and content of architecture is crucial. The objects (buildings) and conditions (space) of architectural production are embedded in the social lifeworld. It follows that if we choose to deny that context, in turn it will shun us as an irrelevance. As long as the architectural centre fixates on polished objects, formal gestations and technologically determined production, it will inevitably get marginalised (in the weak sense of the word). It is only by working through the values set up by Mockbee's strong margins that architecture can once again become relevant.

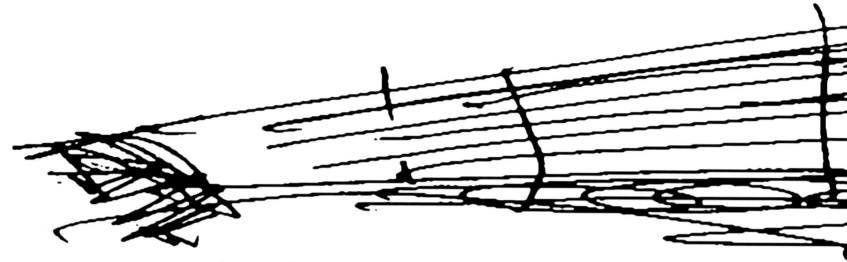

AN ARCHITECT'S UPBRINGING

I know the dirt on an old dairy farm named Yancey in Hale County, Alabama. That soil is different from most that you will find in the black belt. When the earth on Yancey is compact, it is as hard as bedrock. When that ground is pried loose, it is as fine as quartz dust. I know that dirt because Sambo let me build a chapel of it as a thesis project- with a friend called Dirtman and another named Tom. We constructed the Yancey Chapel with anything we could get our hands on – objects collected, salvaged, or dug. The materials cost almost nothing; we, the laborers and designers, were free.

The genesis of the chapel came over a Heineken with Sambo. We were teetering in rocking chairs on the porch of our home at dusk. We lived in an antebellum mansion with no air conditioning in the slow town of Greensboro, Alabama – a teacher and ten students completing a house built of hay bales, the first project of the Rural Studio. Sambo was the big man with a beard who sat at the end of our dinner table – he owned our attention. He triumphed in our discovering new building methods and utilizing old and discarded things. We were in the midst of his first victory - providing a warm dry place for a charming catfish fisherman and his family.

There Sambo and I sat - overlooking an unkempt lawn half the size of a football field. I was comfortable, inspired, and confident in his presence - as I was not always with my peers on that project. I told him that I would like to stay in Greensboro - build something start to finish as a thesis project. He did not hesitate in his response, "a chapel," he said - an inspiration for others, a sacred space. Sambo stood behind my idea, giving it form at that very moment; just as Professor DK Ruth stood behind his back at Auburn University - guarding the Rural Studio, making it happen for us. As our conversation progressed, Sambo was trying to think of the right backer for the chapel: someone with land in the community, who supported Auburn and the studio. He stopped rocking and said, "You should talk to Lemuel Morrison." And so I met with her shortly thereafter. Lemuel's eyes lit up wickedly as I proposed my plan to build a chapel on her land. She whispered to me that her property had a certain magic quality.

It is odd to recall that part of my wish to stay in Greensboro had been "wanting to do my own thing." That desire ultimately led to becoming one of a group of three - building by hand. I found great people to work with - diligent resourceful, people: Tom Tretheway, a man of action, Steve Durden a dreamer. Our team met for several days over Christmas break to shape our ideas and design the Yancey Chapel. We chose a site that overlooks a bluff, unusual to the landscape of Hale County. We presented our base design to the landowner; she seemed pleased. Sambo inquired of us via telephone afterwards. "Is the chapel cool?" "Yes," we answered. "Can you build it?" "No," we replied. "Good!" He reveled in watching students envision things they wanted to create, *then* figuring out how to build them.

Our team finally met the dirt. The three of us dug a rectangular hole in the ground and piled its emptied contents high around the edges. We collected tires from a nearby dump. We rammed the excavated earth into those tires. We pounded them into a running bond pattern around the dugout sanctuary. Thus were born the retaining walls for our chapel. We covered them in chicken wire, then stucco. We began a roof of salvaged hundred-year-old heart pine beams. We added shingles cut from old barn tin. As we worked, we knew what we were willing to try. Sambo knew what would work. He would quietly, unassumingly let us know if we were headed for trouble. He would never give us answers. He moved us forward by wanting us to clear our own hurdles. He inspired us by imparting a sense that we were *doing*, that these creations springing from our hands would generate wonder.

One afternoon back at the house our team sat around the dining room table, paralyzed by indecision. Winter had become spring and we had tire walls and pine rafters, but no roof. We could not resolve the finished roof structure; we could not even agree upon its materials. Sambo dropped in upon our dilemma; he suggested he might give us some help. We begged him not to, but he picked up a piece of paper and started sketching with lightening speed. He was mumbling, "You're running out of time, you're running out of time..." We did not want him to give us the answer, but at the same time, we were intrigued - waiting for the master's illumination.

Finally he handed us the sketch our

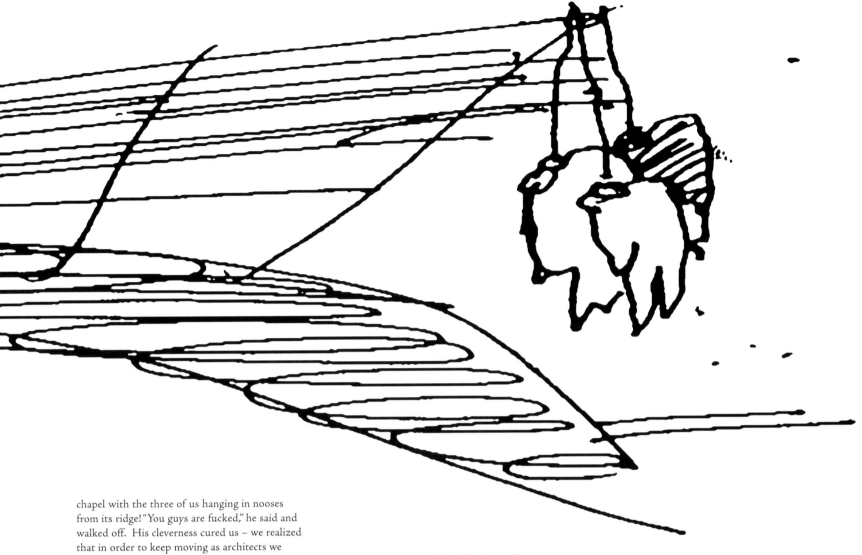

chapel with the three of us hanging in nooses from its ridge! "You guys are fucked," he said and walked off. His cleverness cured us – we realized that in order to keep moving as architects we would have to be willing to be decisive. The next day we finalized the roof structure and agreed to cut shingles of salvage barn tin, rusted into colors that we could never find again.

It is only appropriate that Sambo sketched us tied to our building, as his world was built of people. No matter how well he knew someone he never lost the air of fascination with them. No sooner did he meet someone than he began to watch for their needs. Sambo wove his strengths through anyone that was willing to participate in his grand plan. It was wonderful to know him in a place where he knew his way through the fishponds and the woods, where he was excited by everything that was going on, as a mighty man flown in to save the day. So many deserving people have found themselves in new homes, so many students have found a realm in which to design and build. So many people have been made to feel bold. He taught me the thrill of a group assimilating each of its individual views, of building something with character.

When we finished our chapel Sambo said to us, "Well it's all downhill from here. You've done the best. You'll never be able to beat it." Although I enjoy my career of high residential architecture, my experience under Sambo in the Rural Studio will always be my architectural compass.

Sambo loved the South, he loved architecture, he loved the people of Hale County. With a lifetime's experience of crafting in the vernacular, he began an outreach that was an interpretation of his passions. We find Sambo in the pages of so many books, because he stepped so far beyond what had previously been written. As one enters the Yancey Chapel, one passes a concrete angel gesture. A lovely stream moves through it into the sanctuary. One may not recognize this angel upon first glance – he unobtrusively stands and looks out over the bluff, into the world.

Written by Alice Novak and Ruard Veltman

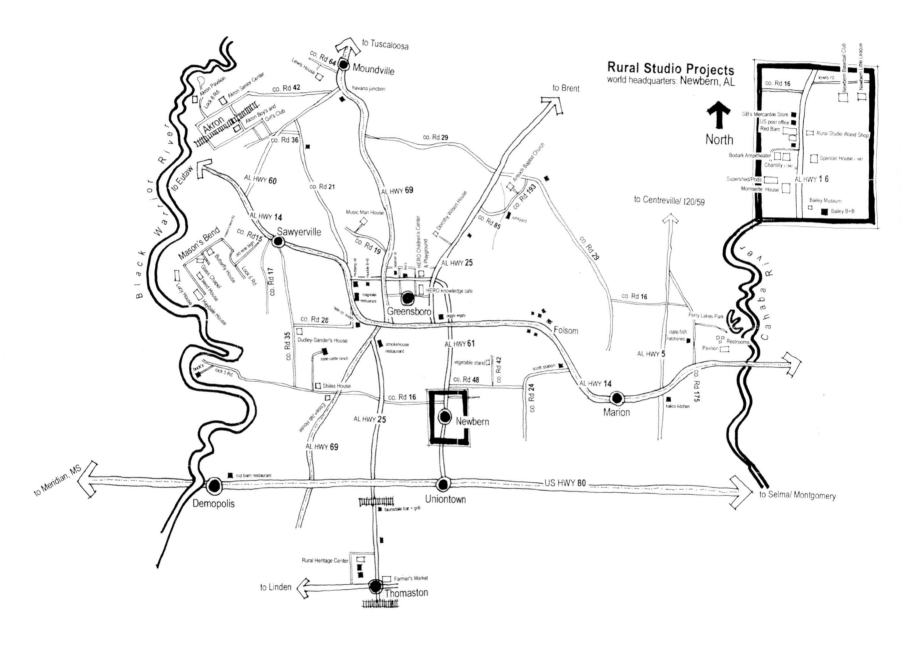

to Tuscaloosa

co. Rd **64** Moundville

to Brent

Rural Studio Projects
world headquarters: Newbern, AL

↑
North

co. Rd **16** lewis rd.
Newbern Baseball Club
Newbern Little League

GB's Mercantile Store
US post office
Red Barn
Rural Studio Wood Shop

Bodark Ampitheater
Chantilly (c. 1907)
Spence House (c. 1907)

Supershed/Pods
Morrisette House
AL HWY **16**
Bailey Museum
Bailey B+B

Akron Pavilion
Lock 8 Rd
Akron Senior Center
co. Rd **42**
Lewis House
havana junction

Akron
Akron Boy's and Girl's Club

co. Rd **29**

co. Rd **36**

AL HWY **60**
co. Rd **21**
AL HWY **69**

AL HWY **14**
Music Man House
Dorothy Wilson House
Antioch Baptist Church
co. Rd **193**

co. Rd **15**
Sawyerville
co. Rd **19**
HERO Children's Center & Playground
junkyard
co. Rd **85**

Mason's Bend
old store sign
Butterfly House
Glass Chapel
Lock 6 Rd
co. Rd **17**

Lucy House
Harris Lewis Rd.
Akron Rd.
Seed House
Haybale House

to Eutaw

Black Warrior River

co. Rd **29**

to Centreville/ I20/59

AL HWY **25**

magnolia restaurant
Greensboro
HERO knowledge cafe

co. Rd **16**

co. Rd **28**
top co. supply
piggly wiggly
Folsom

co. Rd **35**
Dudley-Sander's House
smokehouse restaurant
AL HWY **61**
state fish hatcheries
Pavilion
Restrooms
Perry Lakes Park

black's
lock 5 Rd
state cattle ranch
vegetable stand
co. Rd **42**
AL HWY **5**

Cahaba River

Shiles House
co. Rd **16**
co. Rd **48**
co. Rd **24**
scott station
AL HWY **14**
kalico kitchen
co. Rd **175**

AL HWY **25**
Newbern
Marion

AL HWY **69**

to Meridian, MS
red barn restaurant
US HWY **80**
to Selma/ Montgomery

Demopolis
Uniontown

faunsdale bar + grill

Rural Heritage Center
Farmer's Market

to Linden
Thomaston

Appendix of Rural Studio Projects 2001-2003

Photography by Timothy Hursley

WHEN DAVID MOOS ASKED ME IF I THOUGHT AN APPENDIX OF RECENT PROJECTS TO THE EXHIBITION CATALOGUE WAS A GOOD IDEA, OF COURSE I EAGERLY AGREED. David's idea was to show the Rural Studio projects completed since Sambo's death. However, what I failed to consider in my hasty enthusiasm was the sheer volume of projects, and hence the number of project descriptions I would have to write. In 2002, the Rural Studio completed seven projects; in 2003, we have just completed eleven projects. This equates to eighteen projects completed in eighteen months—virtually a small town.

This achievement alone represents an enormous tribute to Sambo.

It is also a great tribute to the organization that he was responsible for putting in place at the Rural Studio. The Rural Studio's survival is a testament to the fact that Sambo and D. K. Ruth's idea is a great idea, and that great ideas endure. The Rural Studio is also a reflection of a certain spirit and, ten years on, this exhibition, appropriately enough, allows an opportunity to reflect on that spirit.

I think Sambo would be very pleased that the Rural Studio has, to use his words, "moved on." I always found him to be most unsentimental. The Rural Studio was testament to his extraordinary appetite for the future and for the "next battle." In moving on, I think, and hope, that he'd be delighted with the craft of the latest projects. I also think he'd be delighted, but also a little anxious, at their enormous ambition.

In this tenth inspiring year, as well as, reflection on some eighty projects, Sambo's legacy will be guarded and continued. His wife, Jackie, is on the newly formed Rural Studio Advisory Board, and his daughter, Carol, enters the Rural Studio Outreach Program.

As for Hale County, it is hard to fully describe the depth of love and warmth that is felt toward Sambo. He is sorely missed:

We miss him barreling through the West Alabama landscape in his red GMC truck, delighting in this land's natural beauty. According to Sambo, "Morrisette Bottom looks like the South of France"—although of course he had never set foot in France!

We miss him in student critiques, sprinkling "whiffle dust" on the projects and demanding that the projects be "bad," "whacked-out," or at least "real pretty"!

We miss the extraordinary range of ideas and possibilities that he used to talk about. He often talked of how he felt architects only reached their peak at the age of sixty. I can bear witness to the fact that at fifty-seven he was becoming very special and had gained a special confidence.

We miss his wonderful anecdotes and how they would become more elaborate each time he told them. As he suggested "why let the truth get in the way of a good story!"

We miss watching him draw, paint, and sketch. The delight and freedom of expression that he found in these pursuits was an example to us all.

We miss his clarion call "Let's go eat!"—crawfish at Cajohn's, catfish at Bucks, rib sandwiches at Mustang Oil, slabs of ribs at Dreamland in Tuscaloosa (we'd sneak up "into Enemy Territory…under cover of darkness"), crab claws at the Red Barn, breakfast at the Spencer House, and, of course, "Suicide Dogs" at Lou's.

As you can see, with Sambo's passing, the Hale County restaurant economy has taken a big hit!

But, above all, we miss his sense of fun and good humor. Sambo knew how to live life to the full. From good food, to good drink, to great people and stories. In a world of "pretentious" architects and "serious" architecture, he made life, education, and architecture a delight.

We hope to keep his spirit, and therefore the spirit of the Rural Studio, alive. We hope that you witness this spirit in the exhibition.

But this exhibition is a small reflection of Sambo and the Rural Studio. We invite you to come and visit Hale County, to see the place, the work, and the people. It is a place that Sambo loved and that in turn loved Sambo.

And you will find that in Hale County, Sambo is all around.

– *Andrew Freear*

SHILES HOUSE

Hale County, Alabama
2001/2002 Sophomore Year Project

CLIENT:

Ms. Tracy Shiles

STUDENT TEAM (Fall 2002):

Jason Bouthillette, Ben Collins, David Davis, Connely Farr, John Nathan Foust, Daniel Splaingard, Dustin Shue, Mark Wise, Robert Wright, Jr., Blair Bricken, Julieta Collart, Leigh Ann Duncan, Lana Farkas, Lauren Frayer, Lauren Tate Foy, Mona Pedro

(Spring 2003):

David Boettcher, Sloan Flournoy, Philip Hamilton, Kevin Chang-yub Kim, Jonathan Mahorney, Justin Rogers, Jeremy Sargent, Ryan Vernon, Alicia Gjesvold, Allison Kulpa, Jennifer Thompson, Heidi Schattin, Jessica Zenor, Tamika Watts, Mary Helen Neal, Malin Ulmer

OVERVIEW:

Ms. Tracy Shiles, a nurse and the guardian of two young boys, became the recipient of this house because of her efforts to further her education.

The house is an elevated structure incorporating tire construction techniques previously used by the Rural Studio in the Yancey Chapel design. Standing on telephone pole stilts to lift the building out of a wet landscape, the house touches the ground at specific points using the tire structure.

The tires penetrate the interior of the building, creating a winding staircase that wraps around the family room. The entryway signified by a "big roof" is a modified dogtrot form, with the children's rooms and family room on one side and the kitchen, utility room, and mother's room on the other side of the dogtrot.

The striking exterior is clad in oak shingles cut from wooden shipping pallets.

THE LUCY HOUSE

Mason's Bend, Hale County, Alabama
2001/2002 Outreach Studio Project

CLIENT:

Anderson and Lucy Harris

STUDENT TEAM:

Ben Cannard, Philip Crosscup, Floris Keverling Buisman,
Kerry Larkin, J. M. Tate, Marie Richard, Keith Zawistowski

OVERVIEW:

Originally conceived by Samuel Mockbee, the Lucy House is a collaboration of the Rural Studio and a national carpet manufacturer. The house is home to Anderson and Lucy Harris and their three children. Anderson and Lucy are the children of the owners of the Hay Bale and Butterfly houses, also Rural Studio projects.

The 1,200-square-foot house has two pieces. The main room or "family room" contains three children's bedrooms, bathroom, kitchen, and living area. This room is contained by carpet-tiled walls. These walls are built of 24,000 individually stacked carpet tiles that are held in compression by a heavy wooden ring beam. Carpet does not take the roof load, but instead the load is transferred to the foundation through structural metal posts hidden in the carpet wall.

The other major built form is a bedroom for Anderson and Lucy, housed in the crumpled form that sits atop the family's tornado shelter. The tornado shelter also acts as a meditation room and family TV room.

The house is built of carpet tiles salvaged from office buildings throughout the U.S.A. The tiles are older than seven years and therefore have minimal off-gas. They are protected from the elements by the Rural Studio's trademark "big roof." In the future, the carpet company plans to recycle all of its carpet tiles.

AKRON SENIOR CENTER

Akron, Hale County, Alabama
2001/2002 Thesis Project

CLIENT:

Town of Akron, Area Agency on the Aging, Golden Years, Akron Community Leaders

STUDENT TEAM:

Matt Barrett, Jonathan Graves, Breanna Hinderliter, Joe Yeager

OVERVIEW:

By observing the success of the Boys and Girls Club, built in Akron two years previously, community members decided it was time to address the needs of their elderly. A double-fronted 3,500-square-foot country store across the street from the Boys and Girls Club and just off the railroad was chosen to house a senior center.

Not only does the building provide a place for senior citizens of the community to eat a hot, nutritious meal, socialize, and interact with others, but also offers a place for them to participate in recreational activities and programs geared toward the special needs of senior citizens. These activities take place in the glass storefront that wraps around one half of the building.

The second half of the space is a community center for the town. Here, an aircraft-hanger door cranks open and activity spills out onto the street.

ANTIOCH BAPTIST CHURCH

Perry County, Alabama
2001/2002 Thesis Project

CLIENT:

Antioch Baptist Church Congregation

STUDENT TEAM:

Gabe Michaud, Jared Fulton, Marion McElroy, Bill Nauck

OVERVIEW:

The Antioch Baptist Church in northwest Perry County has a small congregation based on four families. With the existing church lacking a restroom and baptismal font, it was losing membership.

Although a romantic little structure, the existing building had major foundation problems, so a decision was made to replace the building. The Rural Studio students charged themselves with using all of the salvageable materials from the original church, including roof and floor joists, wood wall paneling, tongue-and-groove boards, and exterior corrugated metal sheathing. With these materials, the students built a small chapel for the congregation's Sunday services.

The new building has a dramatic sloping roof, held up by hand-built composite metal and wood trusses. The building also forms a retaining wall and water diverter to the cemetery hill. The main view from the sanctuary of the church is through a horizontal window that allows the congregation to be at eye level with the graveyard. The baptismal font is below the baptistery and accessed by a secret tiled stairway.

Architecturally, the building contains two interlocking wrapping forms: one runs north-south and contains the soaring south wall, the ceiling, and the horizontal glass wall. The other wrap runs east-west and forms the baptistery at the west and preacher's room and restroom at the East entrance. The exterior of the building is clad in student-installed galvanized aluminum.

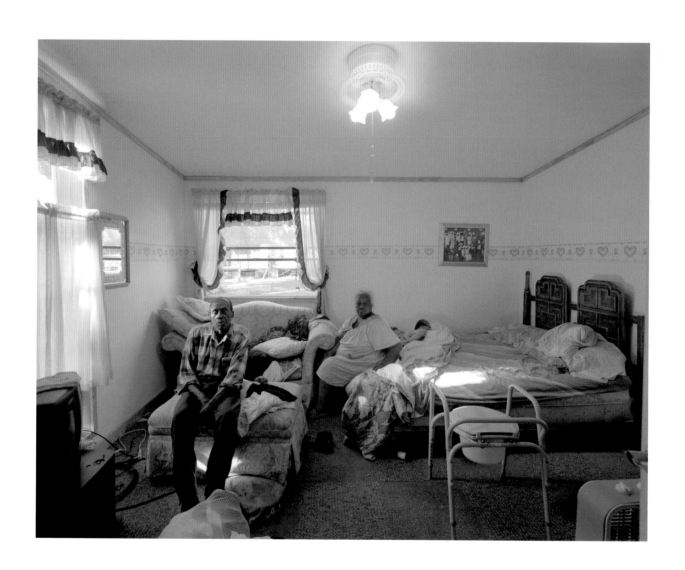

ARCHITECTURAL AMBULANCE

Hale County, Alabama
2001/2002 Thesis Project

CLIENT:

Essie and Jab Williams

STUDENT TEAM:

Jody Touchstone

OVERVIEW:

This project began to look closely at the rural health needs of the aging population throughout Hale County. Jody Touchstone studied the health systems in the area and completed home visits to assess the architectural needs of geriatric patients.

She completed many small projects including a wheelchair ramp and redesign of a door opening. The largest of the projects was a warm, dry room for an elderly couple, Essie and Jab Williams. Jody assessed their immediate emergency needs and designed and built a large multipurpose room and a bathroom with wheelchair-accessible shower. What is remarkable about Jody's addition to Essie and Jab's home is that it is completely accessible from the rest of the house, and yet in the event of the front of the house becoming uninhabitable, they will be able to live in the addition.

The Rural Studio has ambitions to further explore and sustain this project investigation in the future.

HERO KNOWLEDGE CAFÉ

Greensboro, Hale County, Alabama
2001/2002 Thesis Project

CLIENT:

HERO (Hale Empowerment and Revitalization Organization) and the Family Resource Center

STUDENT TEAM:

John McCabe, Andrea Ray, Daniel Sweeney, R. Matt Wilson

OVERVIEW:

This existing single-story shop front was transformed into a state-of-the-art technology center for Greensboro and Hale County.

The building becomes a gateway to the HERO campus and the two glass ends of the building allow you to see the main campus from Main Street. The loft-like appearance: the walls, floor, and ceiling were stripped-down to their original materials and along with few built elements will allow the building to be used in a very flexible manner in the future. HERO works on three-year grant cycles; the building's future function is not easy to predict. While the Community Career Resource Center presently occupies the space, it is expected to become an electronic café where local residents can access the Internet.

The front street canopy and loggia serves to structurally stabilize the masonry façade as well as provide a shading device and entrance sign.

The rear façade, made completely of donated Pella windows, forms a playful formal relationship and connection with the Children's Center on the main HERO campus.

CEDAR PAVILION

Perry Lakes Park, Perry County, Alabama
2001/2002 Thesis Project

CLIENT:

Perry Lakes Board, Perry County Commission

STUDENT TEAM:

Jennifer Bonner, Mary Beth Maness, Nathan Orrison, Anthony Tindill

OVERVIEW:

After being closed for over thirty years, Perry Lakes Park/Barton's Beach was reopened to the people of Perry County in May 2002. The Park is located seven miles northeast of the small town of Marion and is situated on the winding Cahaba River. It provides a place for recreation, fishing, canoeing, birding, walking, and public access to the Cahaba River. Throughout the year, the students had an amazing opportunity to work closely with a board comprised of community leaders including the probate judge, mayor, county commissioner, and Nature Conservancy official.

The cedar pavilion is tucked in amongst the trees and engages with an old picnic area that was made in the 1930s. The roof is a dancing plane that soars to twenty-four feet at its highest point, while the floor surface wraps up to form benches and to make a formal entryway ramp. The entire floor surface is made of cedar donated by a local community member. The students cut the trees out of a cedar thicket and carried them to be milled into lumber in Greensboro.

The pavilion is now being used for community gatherings, catfish frics, family reunions, and an outdoor classroom for Judson College.

MUSIC MAN'S HOUSE

Greensboro, Hale County, Alabama
2002/2003 Sophomore Project

CLIENT:

Jimmy Lee Matthews

STUDENT TEAM: Second-year students and Garth Brown
(Fall 2002):

Erin Aubry, Glen Barfield, Adrienne Brady, John Foshee, Jonathan Fuller, David Garner, Amy Green, Amy Holer, Stephen Long, Nicole McDermott, Gary Miller, Coley Mukahy, Alyson Myer, Amy Owen, Scott Pickens, Katherine Scott, Manley Steale, Alan Stevenson

(Spring 2003):

Carl Dereck Aplin, Joshua Arnett, Robby Austin, Laura Filipek, Amanda Herron, Paul Howard, Angela Hughey, Gabriel Ika, Carrie Jaxon, Shawn Lee Kent, Catherine Liscum, Janice P.Madden, Chance Parrish, Jared Phillips, Monica Starling, Samuel Vines, Trey Wilde, Lauren Willson

OVERVIEW:

A lifetime resident of Greensboro, Alabama, Jimmy Lee Matthews is known to the community as the "Music Man," though he is listed in the phone book as "Mr. Eyes Cancer."

Music Man is single, in his fifties, loves "music, women, and dogs," and has an amazing connection to his land on the "legendary Bates Mill Road." The house of his late mother and uncle still stand on the site, nestled between cedar trees he planted thirty years ago to provide shade. During a storm many years ago, a giant oak tree fell on his trailer and burned his home to the ground. The event forced him to move into fifty square feet of a leaky donated trailer with no plumbing, no ventilation, and inadequate heating.

The project was a full collaboration. The client, instructors, and students from both semesters ate, drank, danced, partied, and prayed together – all in hopes of designing and building a home that would be a vessel for his amazing spirit.

The new structure celebrates Music Man: his curious collecting and recording, his beautiful land, the view, and the cedar trees. It celebrates water, air, fire, and light. Music Man survives.

BOARDWALK AND RESTROOM FACILITIES

Perry Lakes Park, Perry County, Alabama
2002/2003 Thesis Project

CLIENT:

Perry Lakes Board, Perry County Commission

STUDENT TEAM:

Melissa Sullivan, Sarah Dunn Matt Foley, Brannen Park

OVERVIEW:

A continuation of the 2001-2002 Perry Lakes Park thesis project, the efforts of this project focused on establishing a park nucleus, a microcosm of the whole Perry Lakes Park.

The Park nucleus will allow families to come and enjoy all the park has to offer, without having to venture out too far into the unmarked landscape. The project consists of restroom facilities, raised walkways, parking, and information signs.

The pieces of the nucleus have a material palette of cedar, aluminum, and concrete. The walkways are raised to lift people out of the flooding landscape and to connect the parking to the pavilion.

The restrooms consist of a forty-foot-tall tower room with a view to the sky, a horizontal cantilever room that reaches into the landscape to "grab" trees, and a third room "buried" in the septic mound giving views to the earth.

The nucleus is designed to be low maintenance and easily accessed, but also to be a striking signpost feature in the landscape. It will be the most unusual restroom complex in the United States.

NEWBERN LITTLE LEAGUE FIELD

Newbern, Hale County, Alabama
2002/2003 Thesis Project

CLIENT:

Newbern Little League and Town of Newbern

STUDENT TEAM:

Julie Hay, Jason Hunsucker, Patrick Nelson, Jermaine Washington

OVERVIEW:

The Rural Studio was approached by residents and parents truly concerned about the welfare and future of the children in Newbern. They felt that many of the problems associated with the socio-economic conditions of the area could be helped with an inspirational and well-built Little League baseball field. The children's needs included: a safe environment for after-school activities, positive role models, an organized program where children can gain a sense of accomplishment, and a venue where they can work towards sports scholarships.

As a consequence, the Rural Studio approached Baseball Tomorrow, the philanthropic arm of Major League Baseball and the Major League Baseball Player's Association and received funding for this project.

The field was carved from a piece of sloping ground on property donated to the town and the Little League by the estate of Mr. Robert Walthall. The sculpting of the land was made possible using the latest catfish pond excavation technology. The backstop is a series of semicircular hoops that cling to the ground forming a protective "slinky" for the viewing audience. The slinky will be sheathed in catfish net. The lights for the field were also donated.

Our hope is that a new field for the newly formed association will provide a fostering environment for youth sports and that it will enable a wonderful tradition to continue and perhaps eventually produce a young Frank Thomas or Bo Jackson.

RURAL STUDIO GREAT HALL

Newbern, Hale County, Alabama
2002/2003 Thesis Project

CLIENT:

Auburn University Rural Studio

STUDENT TEAM:

Matt Christopher, Clark Gollotte, Kris Johnson, Bert Mitchum

OVERVIEW:

At the Rural Studio, the evening dinner used to be the time for students and faculty to come together to share food, ideas, and the day's events. In the last five years, the Rural Studio has outgrown the old dining room and replaced it with a scattered collection of disconnected spaces. This has resulted in a level of informality and fracturing of what used to be the "family dinner." The aim of the Great Hall is to restore a sense of ceremony and formality to the Rural Studio dinners and to once again seat everyone under one roof and at one table.

The structure, which is adjacent to the Morrisette House, is reminiscent and complimentary of the super shed pod area: a large "building within a building."

It will have large sliding doors that open to allow cross-ventilation and views to the Morrisette backyard.

RURAL HERITAGE
FOUNDATION HEADQUARTERS

Thomaston, Marengo County, Alabama
2002-2003 Thesis Project

CLIENT:

Rural Heritage Foundation, City of Thomaston

STUDENT TEAM:

Katie Bryan, John David Caldwell, Emily McGlohn, Walker Renneker

OVERVIEW:

Following the receipt of a HUD grant, the Rural Heritage Foundation invited the Rural Studio to renovate an abandoned home economic school building to be its new headquarters.

The renovation and rejuvenation will provide for a community art and crafts gallery, pepper jelly-making kitchen, and a gift shop. The facility will also include vegetable cleaning and Town meeting rooms and a new outdoor gathering space. The scope of the project means that it will continue over two years with two separate thesis groups.

Located in the middle of town, the project aspires to bring jobs and economic development to the area.

ORGANIC FARMER'S STAND

Perry County, Alabama
2002/2003 Outreach Studio Project

CLIENT:

Willie Nell and James Avery

STUDENT TEAM:

Cynthia Connolly

OVERVIEW:

In addition to providing Willie Nell and James Avery with a unique place to wash and sell vegetables, the stand is also an artwork that serves as a local landmark and gathering place. Cynthia employed local Alabama artists to help with the design and marketing of this project.

Butch Anthony, an Alabama folk artist, designed the walls of the stand with his "hog-wire" fencing using found objects. Amos Kennedy, a letter press printer and book artist designed and printed promotional posters for the stand. The posters were distributed throughout Tuscaloosa, Perry, Marengo, and Hale counties listing the days and times of eight different farmer's markets, including this one.

Cynthia also employed area basket makers Estelle and Freda Jackson to make and display baskets for sale at the stand.

UTILITY NOW!
BICYCLE STREET SWEEPERS

York, Alabama
2002/2003 Outreach Studio Project

CLIENT:

City of York

STUDENT TEAM:

Richard Saxton

OVERVIEW:

The municipal WORKSHOP and the project UTILITY NOW! is the concept of Rural Studio Outreach student and artist Richard Saxton and a collaboration of the city of York, Alabama, the Coleman Center for the Arts, and Auburn University's Rural Studio Outreach Program. The municipal WORKSHOP developed after York, Alabama's mayor, Carolyn Mitchell-Gosa, invited suggestions for a creative way to solve a current civic issue. The city of York's Public Works Department lacked equipment and transportation necessary for city work crews to complete their duties.

Richard Saxton responded to the request by developing the municipal WORKSHOP in January of 2003 to work with York's Parks and Recreation street crew developing pedal-powered street-sweepers and utility tricycles and bicycles.

The municipal WORKSHOP was located in York's municipal building, allowing Mr. Saxton to create public artwork, demonstrations, and lectures while working side by side with the city employees doing their duties. This project will foster a consciously designed municipality, creative solutions to civic problems, and an air of inspiration and creativity in Alabama's Black Belt.

SUNSHINE SCHOOL
CHILDREN'S THEATER PROJECT

Newbern, Hale County, Alabama
2002/2003 Outreach Studio Project

CLIENT:

The community of Newbern, Auburn University Rural Studio

STUDENT TEAM:

Garth Brown

OVERVIEW:

Rural Studio Outreach student Garth Brown executed improvements to the Rural Studio's outdoor Bodark Amphitheater in Newbern. He collaborated with local citizens and students from the Sunshine Elementary School to produce two plays in the amphitheater for the local community and for the Rural Studio Pig Roast graduation celebration.

OLE MAE'S PORCH

Greensboro, Alabama
2002/2003 Outreach Studio Project

CLIENT:

Ole Mae Warren

STUDENT TEAM:

Lucy Begg

OVERVIEW:

Rural Studio Outreach student Lucy Begg researched the ubiquitous house trailer as a rural housing type and proposed and constructed an extensive porch for the trailer of a Depot Street neighborhood resident.

The porch was built atop the steel chassis of an abandoned trailer found on site, demonstrating how parts of uninhabitable trailers can be reused to extend and open the living areas of usually introverted mobile homes.

"UNCLE HENRY'S HOUSE":
A HOUSE FOR NANCY

Newbern, Perry County, Alabama
2002/2003 Neck-down Project

CLIENT:

Nancy Henry

PROJECT TEAM:

Ben Cannard, Nancy Henry, Greg Hinton

OVERVIEW:

The Rural Studio often undertakes works known as "neck-down" projects (they require no brain). These include much-needed services such as rebuilding roofs, wheelchair ramps, front porches, and fixing every-day leaks. Ravaged by kidney failure, Uncle Henry died and left a young widow in need of a home. The new home was initially to be based on an abandoned trailer-chassis designed by a faculty member. However, subsequent to Uncle Henry's death, a small house on an adjoining site became available that the Rural Studio proceeded to renovate.

   The project soon required more than "neck-down" involvement. Voluntarily taken on by Ben Cannard, a former Outreach student, assisted by Nancy Henry and her son-in-law, Greg Hinton, the little house has turned into a series of delightful, and playful, multi-colored rooms.

LEE COUNTY AIDS ALABAMA HOUSE

Lee County, Alabama
2002-2003

CLIENT:

AIDS Alabama, East Alabama AIDS Outreach and their patients

PROJECT TEAM:

Travis Burke, Erik Lindholm, Seth Rodwell, Jason Schmidt

OVERVIEW:

In 2002-03, Rural Studio completed its first project in Lee County, the home county of Auburn University. The project was a collaborative effort with Auburn University's Social Work Program, AIDS Alabama, and East Alabama AIDS Outreach (EAAO). Four thesis students designed and built a 1,400-square-foot community residence for individuals living with HIV/AIDS and in need of supportive services. A picturesque half-acre site provides permanent housing for three individuals and was constructed with their specific social and medical needs in mind. EAAO provided the property and program support for the structure and residents.

The Lee County project is complex and the design was a challenge. The house includes three bedrooms, three and a half bathrooms, and is wheelchair-accessible. A community area, to be used for programs and events that involve nonresidents, was essential. After researching healing gardens and the effects that they have on the human spirit, the student design team decided that a garden plan would direct the entire design initiative. The floor plan opens up to the garden at every opportunity, providing pleasant views. Some of the walls from the main house extend out into the garden forming comfortable places to relax. A barbecue pit sits at the end of one wall.

In spirit with the garden, the design is also effective in keeping with the aesthetics of Lee County. The overall shape and construction techniques of the house are reminiscent of a typical barn. The house is a post-and-beam construction type that uses hay bales covered with stucco as in-fill. As a design team, the students kept the client at the forefront of the decision process. The project is simple in nature and it relates well to the people who will inhabit the house.

SAMUEL MOCKBEE

Samuel Mockbee, a fifth-generation Mississippian, was born on December 23, 1944, in Meridian. He graduated from Auburn University's College of Architecture, Design and Construction in 1974. After practicing on his own and with Thomas Goodman, he formed a partnership with Coleman Coker in 1983. The firm of Mockbee Coker acquired a reputation for designs that fused traditional Southern architecture with the language of high modernism. In 1993, with his friend and fellow Auburn University professor D. K. Ruth, Mockbee founded the Rural Studio, making pedagogy the conceptual foundation of his architecture. Among the many accolades that Mockbee received for his work at the Rural Studio, in 2000 he was awarded a "genius" grant from the MacArthur Foundation. Mockbee died on December 30, 2001, of complications from leukemia.

CONTRIBUTORS' BIOGRAPHIES

JOE ADAMS is an award-winning playwright, a newspaper humor columnist, a book author, and a poet "on a particularly good day." He is director of America. Oh, Yes! folk art galleries. He is on the national advisory board of The Folk Art Society of America and on the board of The Palm Key Institute. He has also served on the President's Advisory Committee for the Arts. He claims that he advised President Clinton to "buy anything with a picture of Elvis on it." Adams is currently actually putting together a collection of Elvis folk art for the new Clinton Presidential Library.

G. WILLIAMSON "B.B." ARCHER, Architect: Wife Sally, three Children. 1972 Architectural graduate USL. Owner Archer Architects, Meridian, Miss. 1989 MS. AIA President, Foundation President 1990. Advisory Council Member MSU College of Architecture and the Auburn Rural Studio. Has been published in Architecture Magazine, Southern Accents, Southern Living, Mississippi Magazine and the Mississippi Architect. Published Cookbook: *Archer's Cajun Cookery*. Continuing education Cajun cooking instructor: Meridian Public Schools and Meridian Community College since 1986.

STEVE BADANES is the Howard. S. Wright Professor of Architecture at University of Washington and a partner in Jersey Devil, a group of architects, artists and inventors committed to the interdependence of design and building. Jersey Devil work is known for energy efficiency and innovative use of materials and has been profiled in the recent monograph: "Devil's Workshop – 25 years of Jersey Devil Architecture." He has been involved with the Rural Studio as graduation speaker, and on an annual basis as lecturer, reviewer and consultant.

RANDY BATES was born in Meridian, Miss., and lived there until he was eighteen. He wrote *Rings: On the Life and Family of a Southern Fighter* and teaches English and nonfiction writing at the University of New Orleans.

JENNIFER BONNER, a graduate of Auburn University's School of Architecture, had the privilege of building her thesis project at the Rural Studio. Along with three other teammates she designed and built a community pavilion out of local cedar wood for the people of Perry County. Upon graduation in the Spring of 2002, she was asked to join the faculty and staff of the Rural Studio and become the Clerk of Works. She was the second Clerk of Works in history at the Rural Studio.

DAVID BUEGE teaches in the College of Architecture at Mississippi State University.

WILLIAM CHRISTENBERRY was born in Tuscaloosa, Ala., in 1936. He attended the University of Alabama where he received a BFA and MA in Painting in 1959. After several years as an Instructor at the University, he went to New York City. In 1962 Christenberry was appointed Assistant Professor of Art at Memphis State University. In 1968, he and his wife, Sandra, moved to Washington, DC, where he has taught advanced drawing and painting at the Corcoran College of Art and Design since the late 1960s. Christenberry's works – which span the media of drawing, painting, sculpture and photography – is owned by and exhibited in museums throughout the United States and Europe.

JOSH C. COOPER, a custom residential designer, received his Bachelor's Degree of Architecture from Auburn University in 1997. Cooper worked for Frank McDonald Architects in Chattanooga, Tennessee from 1998-2001. In the winter of 2001, Cooper started his own design studio, JCC Design. Cooper participated in the Auburn Rural Studio's second year program in 1993, where he helped develop and build the Bryant (Hay Bale) House.

ANDREA OPPENHEIMER DEAN is the author of *Rural Studio: Samuel Mockbee and an Architecture of Decency* (2002), *Centerbrook2* (1997) and *Bruno Zevi: On Modern Architecture* (1983). Formerly executive editor of *Architecture*, she is a contributing editor of *Architectural Record* and *Preservation* magazines.

PAULA DEITZ is editor of *The Hudson Review*, a magazine of literature and the arts published in New York City. As a cultural critic, she writes about art, architecture, design and landscape design and is a regular contributor to *The New York Times*. She has authored several catalogue essays for museum exhibitions and is currently writing a book entitled *Thibaut's Heart* to discover, by retracing the route of the thirteenth-century poet Thibaut de Champagne, how contemporary France lives with its medieval past.

BILL DOOLEY is a painter, the director of the Sarah Moody Gallery of Art and presently serves as chairman of the Department of Art at the University of Alabama. He joined the department after serving as gallery manager at the Knight Gallery in Charlotte, North Carolina. He holds degrees from Georgia Southern College and the University of South Carolina.

JOHN FORNEY is a native Alabamian, an architect with his own practice in Birmingham, and adjunct faculty at Auburn University's Rural Studio.

ANDREW FREEAR, from Yorkshire, England, is Associate Professor at Auburn University. With the untimely death of Samuel Mockbee and the retirement of D. K. Ruth, Freear is now Co-Director of the Rural Studio in Newbern, Alabama. Educated at the Polytechnic of Central London and the Architectural Association, London, he has practiced extensively in London and Chicago, and taught design studio for five years at the University of Illinois at Chicago. He moved to Alabama in 1998 where his main role, aside from directing the program, is thesis project advisor to fifth-year undergraduate students.

FRANK GEHRY has built an architectural career that has spanned four decades and produced public and private buildings throughout the world. In *The New York Times* in November, 1989, architecture critic Paul Goldberger wrote that Mr. Gehry's "buildings are powerful essays in primal geometric form and... materials, and from an aesthetic standpoint they are among the most profound and brilliant works of architecture of our time." His work has earned Mr. Gehry nearly all of the most significant awards in the architectural field, including the Pritzker Prize, the American Institute of Architects Gold Medal, and the National Medal of Arts.

LUCY HARRIS lives in Mason's Bend, Ala., with her husband Anderson, and their four children, Shahrie, Andreanio, Anderson Jr., and Lov Princess Zakekey. She is the daughter of Shepard and Alberta Bryant, clients and recipients of the Rural Studio's first house, the Bryant (Hay Bale) House. In addition, her husband's parents are Anderson and the late Ora Lee Harris, who reside in the Harris (Butterfly) House. Lucy is a member of the Last Day Gospel Church Akron, Ala., where she serves as youth pastor teaching and mentoring the children of congregation. She works full-time as a Certified Nurses' Assistant (C.N.A.) at Moundville Health and Rehabilitation, LLC, caring for senior citizens.

TIMOTHY HURSLEY began his career as an architectural photographer in Detroit, in 1971. He established his own studio in Little Rock, Ark., in 1982. He was the recipient of The American Institute of Architects Honor Award in 1990. He has recently co-authored the book *Rural Studio: Samuel Mockbee and an Architecture of Decency* (2002). His most recent book is *Brothels of Nevada: Candid Views of America's Legal Sex Industry* published by Princeton Architectural Press (2003).

ROBERT IVY, FAIA, is Editor in Chief of the *Architectural Record*, a position he has held since 1996. Previously, Ivy had pursued parallel careers: as an architect with an active practice and as a critic for national publications. Ivy is currently a fellow of the American Institute of Architects, the Philippine Institute of Architects, the Institute for Urban Design, a former regent of the American Architectural Foundation, and a peer reviewer for the U.S. General Services Administration. Ivy holds degrees from the University of the South, where he majored (with honors) in English; and from Tulane University, where he received a degree in architecture.

BRUCE LANIER is a resident of Birmingham, Ala. He worked as a Rural Studio student on the Yancey Chapel (briefly), and the Spencer House porch restoration. In the summer of 2000 he and four other students completed the Thomaston Farmer's Market. Currently, he works for Krumdieck A+I Design, an architecture firm in Birmingham. He has a wife, two children (by the time of this printing), and a gas-powered leaf blower.

KERRY LARKIN was a Rural Studio Outreach student in 2001-2002 and worked on The Lucy House with six other students. After her year at the Rural Studio, she stayed in Hale County to work for HERO (Hale Empowerment Revitalization Organization) teaching G.E.D. classes. In addition, she opened Greensboro's first yoga studio. She has a Bachelor of Architecture degree from Penn State. Starting in the fall of 2003, she will teach design classes at the Charter High School for Architecture and Design in Philadelphia.

WILLIAM LEVINSON is a former magazine columnist and television and film writer. He is currently working on a book about Sambo Mockbee entitled *A Form For Thinking: Sambo Mockbee and the Legacy of the Rural Studio*. He lives in Los Angeles.

ATELIER VAN LIESHOUT (AVL) is a multi-disciplinary company that operates internationally in the field of contemporary art, design and architecture. AVL was founded in 1995 by Joep van Lieshout. The name Atelier Van Lieshout emphasizes the fact that the works of art do not stem solely from the creative brain of Joep van Lieshout, but are produced by a creative team. The works of art are practical, uncomplicated and substantial and include sculpture, furniture, bathrooms and mobile home units as well as complete architectural refurbishments. In 2001 Atelier Van Lieshout realized AVL-Ville, a "free state" in the port of Rotterdam, Holland.

BRUCE LINDSEY is Professor and Head of the School of Architecture at Auburn University and along with Andrew Freear is the Co-Director of the Rural Studio. He recently completed the book *Digital Gehry: Material Resistance Digital Construction* (2002). He has extensive experience in universal and sustainable design and has written and lectured widely on the role of digital technology and design. He has received numerous awards for his design work including several AIA design awards. He received his Masters degree in art from the University of Utah and his Masters degree in architecture from Yale University.

LUCY R. LIPPARD is a writer and activist who has published twenty books on contemporary art and cultural studies, including *Mixed Blessings: New Art in a Multicultural America* (1990), *The Lure of the Local: Senses of Place in a Multi-Centered Society* (1997), and *On the Beaten Track: Tourism, Art and Place* (1999). She lives in Galisteo, New Mexico, where she is the founding editor of the seven-year-old monthly community newsletter, *El Puente de Galisteo*.

BEATRIZ MILHAZES was born in Rio de Janeiro in 1960. She has exhibited her work internationally for the past decade in solo gallery exhibitions in Caracas, Los Angeles, New York, Madrid, Amsterdam, Paris and London. She has participated in the Carnegie International, Pittsburgh (1995), the XXIV Bienal Internacional de São Paulo, São Paulo (1998), Projects 70, Museum of Modern Art, New York (2000), and most recently represented Brazil at La Biennale di Venezia (2003). He first solo exhibition in an American museum was held at the Birmingham Museum of Art (2001).

DAVID MOOS is Curator of Modern and Contemporary Art at the Birmingham Museum of Art.

RUSHTON PATTERSON and JAMES PATTERSON were born and have lived most of their lives in Memphis, TN. They are presently in business together with a medical practice founded by their father, Rushton E. Patterson. The brothers have always been avid collectors. James focuses primarily on contemporary art and historic photography. Rushton collects pre-Columbian art, Peruvian and Bolivian textiles, and American craft pieces. The family jointly purchased a lot on Pickwick Lake in 1993 close to their country home, which is next to Shiloh National Military Park, Tenn. On this spectacular plot of land Samuel Mockbee, in partnership with Coleman Coker, created a house that was as much an art commission as work of architecture.

RICHARD I. PIGFORD, AIA, is a Founding Partner of ArchitectureWorks, LLP. The Birmingham-based firm's work in adaptive re-use, residential, educational, religious and sustainable projects has been recognized for design excellence by the American Institute of Architects local and state components. Pigford is the past chair of the Auburn University School of Architecture Advisory Council and is a recipient of the Distinguished Service award from that institution's School of Architecture. He received a Bachelor of Architecture from Auburn University where he was a classmate of Samuel Mockbee.

CHARLES REEVE is an art historian and art critic who has published widely on modern and contemporary art. His historical writings focus on the intellectual history of the visual arts, while his criticism primarily addresses contemporary developments in art and literature. He lives in Atlanta, where he is editor-in-chief of *Art Papers*.

LARRY RINDER is the Anne and Joel Ehrenkranz Curator of Contemporary Art at the Whitney Museum of American Art. He was chief curator of the 2002 Whitney Biennial, in which Samuel Mockbee the Rural Studio were included. Before his arrival at the Whitney, Rinder was director of the CCAC Institute at the California College of Arts and Crafts, San Francisco and Oakland, California. Prior to this, he was curator for twentieth-century art and MATRIX curator at the Berkeley Art Museum.

District Judge WILLIAM A. RYAN, a native of Hale County, Alabama, is married and the father of three. He has earned engineering and law degrees from The University of Alabama. Before becoming judge in 1987, he was a lawyer, a banker and data processing manager. Ryan serves as Chairman of the Board of West Alabama Youth Services, Inc. and HERO (Hale Empowerment Revitalization Organization). He is member of various state and local boards including the Alabama Department of Youth Services, Voices for Alabama's Children, Children's Trust Fund, and the Administrative Board of Moundville United Methodist Church.

JAY SANDERS attended Auburn University. He was a thesis student at the Rural Studio and since graduating, he served one year as the Rural Studio's Clerk of Works. He has since been appointed the Instructor of the Second Year Studio. He is co-founder of the Beacon Street Studios, a "homespun artistic movement." He is currently working on an untitled Sambo Mockbee documentary film with Sam Wainwright Douglas.

JEREMY TILL and SARAH WIGGLESWORTH are architects and educators based in London. They are both partners in Sarah Wigglesworth Architects, best known for their award-winning project 9 Stock Orchard Street (The Straw House and Quilted Office). Their extensive publications include *Architecture and the Everyday* (1998), which published Samuel Mockbee's writing for the first time in the United Kingdom. Till and Wigglesworth are Professors of Architecture at the University of Sheffield, where Till is also Head of School.

GAIL TRECHSEL is the R. Hugh Daniel Director of the Birmingham Museum of Art.

RUARD VELTMAN grew up in the American South, where his Dutch family settled when he was a young child. He was one of Samuel Mockbee's students in the first two years of the Rural Studio. Along with Steve Durden and Tom Tretheway, Ruard created the Yancey Chapel. He had also helped complete the Bryant (Hay Bale) House. After graduating from Auburn, Ruard began a career in high residential design–working for McAlpine Tankersley Architecture in Montgomery, Ala., for seven years. He and Ken Pursley have since formed Pursley Veltman Architecture in Charlotte, North Carolina. The firm works in a variety of historical styles. ■

Mockbee